I0759528

Mundane MAGIC

Mundane MAGIC

A Lazy Witch's Guide
to Hacking Your Brain,
Building a Daily Practice,
and Getting Stuff Done

Molly Donlan

RODALE
NEW YORK

Rodale Books
An imprint of Random House
A division of Penguin Random House LLC
1745 Broadway, New York, NY 10019
rodalebooks.com | randomhousebooks.com
penguinrandomhouse.com

Mundane Magic is not intended to be a substitute for professional medical advice, diagnosis, or treatment. Always seek the advice of your physician or other qualified health provider with any questions you may have regarding a medical condition or treatment.

Library of Congress Cataloging-in-Publication Data
Names: Donlan, Molly author
Title: Mundane magic / Molly Donlan.
Description: First edition. | New York, NY: Rodale, [2026] | Includes appendix.
Identifiers: LCCN 2025033908 (print) | LCCN 2025033909 (ebook) |
ISBN 9780593980347 hardcover | ISBN 9780593980354 ebook
Subjects: LCSH: Magic | Housekeeping—Miscellanea |
Self-help techniques—Miscellanea
Classification: LCC BF1623.H67 D66 2026 (print) | LCC BF1623.H67 (ebook)
LC record available at https://lccn.loc.gov/2025033908
LC ebook record available at https://lccn.loc.gov/2025033909

Printed in the United States of America

3rd Printing

First Edition

Book Team: Production editor: Cara DuBois • Managing editor: Allison Fox • Production manager: Angela McNally • Proofreaders: Alissa Fitzgerald, Anya Getschel, Catherine Mallette, Zora O'Neill, Tess Rossi

Book design by Alexis Flynn

Illustrations by Alaina Borst

Adobe Stock illustrations: piixypeach (title-page pattern), kossovskiy (background texture), Foxy Fox (moon phase border)

The authorized representative in the EU for product safety and compliance is Penguin Random House Ireland, Morrison Chambers, 32 Nassau Street, Dublin D02 YH68, Ireland. https://eu-contact.penguin.ie

For Sarah & Madison—
who both continue to remind me of my own Magic.

Contents

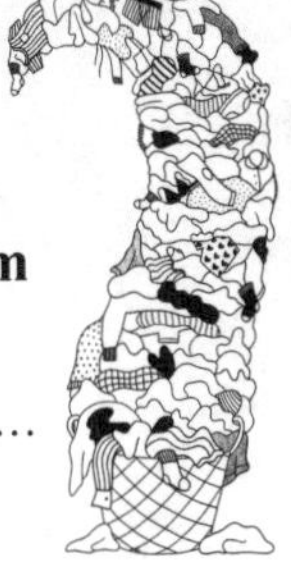

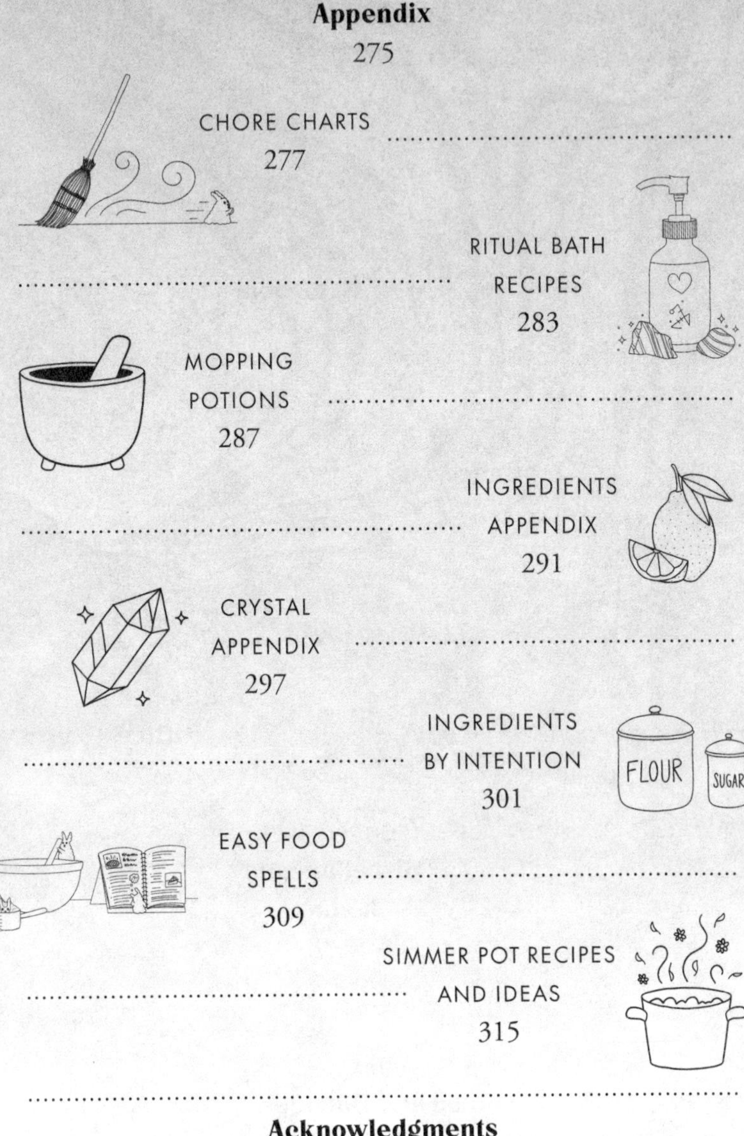
FLOUR
SUGAR
S

Mundane MAGIC

Introduction

My Story

There it was, at the bottom of my purse, shining back up at me. There is NO way this glittery rock turned my luck around, unless . . .

The year is 2015, and if you told me that a decade later I'd be writing a book about Magic I would have laughed in your face and assumed you meant some *Hocus Pocus,* Harry Potter remake. But Magic saved me. To me, Magic is so much more than just waving a wand, saying *bippity boppity,* and wishing on a star (or whatever TV tells you it is). Magic is a path home to your authentic self.

When I was diagnosed with ADHD in elementary school, I resigned myself to being a messy, disorganized person for life. I assumed I would always struggle to keep my room clean, go to bed at a reasonable hour, or feed myself three basic meals a day. As a child, this wasn't a huge issue, but once I grew into adulthood and took on an all-consuming career as an advocate for survivors of sexual violence, shit began to hit the fan.

At twenty-three, I found myself living with two strangers I'd met on Craigslist, in an apartment without heat, suffering from a consistent state of no-good-very-bad-days.

I had the chronic pain of an eighty-year-old (according to my doctors), absolutely zero hobbies outside of work, low self-esteem, anxiety, and a schedule as messy as my car (which could have been compared to a drive-thru restaurant's trash can). And to top it all off, we had fleas. FLEAS!! Needless to say, I was in a slump.

So when my roommate suggested smoke cleansing the apartment to banish my bad luck, I was willing to try anything, even if it sounded like bullshit. We paraded down to the local metaphysical shop to find a bundle of herbs. I walked through the shelves of divination books, tarot cards, and incense sticks that claimed they'd call in the love of my life. Rolling my eyes, I found myself drawn to the back of the space, looking through a bin of pretty rocks.

That's when it caught my attention: a glittery rock that I couldn't get out of my head. I picked it up and it felt like it was meant to be in my hand. I read the tiny slip of paper next to it that said, "Pyrite—shields negative energy, prevents bad luck." I thought to myself, *What the hell—I'll buy it because it's shiny*. Then I walked up to the register, paid the nice lady, tucked it away in my purse, and promptly forgot about it.

We smoke cleansed the apartment and spent the day creating an all-natural floor cleaner that could ward away fleas—including lemon for cleansing and rosemary to banish them. As an ADHD girlie who avoids mopping at all costs, I'd never had more fun cleaning my space.

Several weeks later, my life was unrecognizable. My job title changed to a position I always dreamed of working in, I found myself surrounded by friends and entrenched in the local theater community, our landlord FINALLY agreed to hire a professional to remove the fleas, and those Craigslist strangers became my best friends to this day. On a beautiful spring afternoon, as I cleaned out my purse, that pyrite tumbled out. I thought to myself, *There's no way this worked. Unless . . .*

That's when I started to become curious about Magic. Not fully convinced, of course; it took years of experimentation and discovery to overcome twenty-plus years of skepticism. But slowly I started to uncover links between what I understood about science and spirituality—namely the nervous system, the brain, and mindfulness practices. I used Magical tools like crystals, mindfulness, and cleansing energy to make the blah of life more exciting and to serve as life rafts through everyday turbulence. As I started to realize that science and Magic go hand in hand, my skepticism dissolved. I started integrating Magic into my life, and I found myself in awe of these practices and their transformative power over everyday life.

Ultimately, what I discovered along the way was this: **Magic is everywhere.** You can choose to look for it, or you can choose to ignore it. But the more you zoom in on micro moments of Magic in your life, the more it expands into your awareness.

Magic doesn't have to be some hokey spell with a rhyming incantation; it can be simply noticing how delicious your coffee tastes in the morning. Magic can be intentionally choosing your outfit based on what energy you want to embody for the day. Magic can be a tool to make mopping a little more enjoyable.

What you focus on expands, and most of us focus on the negative. We see the stress of work, the lack of money, the mess in the nooks and crannies of our homes. Your brain is wired to zoom in on these things because it wants to keep you alive. The more it focuses on the negative, the more threats it can evade that might harm you. But a lot of us get locked into this negativity and struggle to dig ourselves out of it.

Magic doesn't remove this negativity because it can't eliminate the stress of life. Instead, Magic balances out the negative. It can help you ride the wave of life's stresses rather than getting pulled down by the undertow.

Magic allows you to see the stress of work AND not let it consume your life.

Magic allows you to see the lack of money AND come up with creative ways to invite abundance into your life.

Magic allows you to see the mess AND the fun that created it.

Therefore: Magic is mindfulness. Magic is motivation. Magic is empowerment. This book is designed to help you reconnect with the Magic that is already within you. Because, my friend, the truth is that **YOU are the Magic. (More on that later!)**

The more you recognize the Magic in daily life, the more it expands, and the more you realize you can create Magic whenever you want. And because we like feeding two worms with one apple, we can use Magic to convince ourselves to actually do those annoying chores you keep avoiding.

Introducing Mundane Magic

There's a tiger chasing me and its name is "folding laundry." You see, once I pull my clothes from the dryer I know it will take me less than ten minutes to do and yet my cute little brain wants to do literally anything else. So the laundry expands, I dig for clean socks every morning, and the baskets pile up. Come Friday, I have four hampers and a chair covered in clean laundry. Now my brain is certain it will take all day to tackle this project, so I sit and stare at the mess feeling worse and worse about it, unable to find the motivation to just get started.

Sound familiar? If you're like me, everyday tasks like folding laundry can feel impossible even when we realistically *know* they aren't. Maybe you're a squiggly-brained overachiever with ADHD and wayyy too many novelty T-shirts (guilty!), or maybe you have 17,381 things on your to-do list and taking care of yourself keeps getting bumped to the next day (and the next . . .), or maybe you have a houseful of people who need your energy—**no matter who you are, you inevitably struggle with doing "the thing," and Mundane Magic is a life hack for making "the thing" more doable** (and dare I say, sometimes FUN!). In particular for those of us with neurodivergent cognitive functioning, our brains struggle with task initiation, aka the "get started" motivation needed to begin a mundane task. Much like a car needs gasoline to run, you need that initial motivation to kick off the momentum. With ADHD, that motivation often comes in the form of novelty. After all, ADHD brains don't struggle with doing everything (hyperfixate much?), just things that we don't *want* to do—specifically, mundane or repetitive tasks. Your brain will avoid those like a tiger chasing you through the jungle, making washing the dishes feel like an overwhelming chore bent on ruining your mood.

Enter: Mundane Magic.

For me, Magic has become a life hack to kick-start my motivation, add the novelty needed to get shit done, and empower me to feel more in control of my day. **Making a boring chore Magical adds a level of novelty and dopamine to the things that need to get done, so you actually end up doing them.**

What is Mundane Magic exactly?

Mundane Magic was born from my fascination with nervous system regulation and my need to vacuum up dog hair around my house. After spending nine years supporting survivors of sexual violence through various nonprofits, I learned quite a bit about how our brains function when under stress. There are two sides to your nervous system: your stress response, designed for survival, when your brain thinks a tiger is literally chasing you; and then your relaxation response, the side where your brain can relax and replenish itself. Your brain, because it wants to keep you alive, doesn't know the difference between a tiger chasing you and your WiFi buffering for a little bit too long before an important meeting. Your brain assumes all stress is a tiger until you prove it otherwise. We'll get deeper into the nervous system in Chapter 1 but what you really need to know is this:

If there were a real-life tiger in your house, you wouldn't stop to fold your laundry.

So the first step in finding the motivation to do these chores has to be reassuring your brain that it is safe. We do this by implementing mindfulness techniques and intention setting as the premise for Mundane Magic.

Once your brain isn't freaking the heck out, it needs some of that "get started" gas to actually do the thing you've been avoiding. What's the easiest way to gas up your brain? Introduce novelty—make the task more fun or interesting and watch the barriers to your motivation drop away.

In essence, Mundane Magic is making your everyday tasks a little bit more witchy so you actually do them. **Whether it's a meditative technique, spell casting, or energy healing your space, this book explores a variety of Magical practices using household items to initiate your motivation and infuse a bit of Magic into your daily life.**

When I started working from home, I thought, *Oh, my house will be SO clean all the time, I can just clean a little every day.* Go ahead and laugh, because that obviously didn't happen. As the dog hair piled up on my stairs and the dishes overwhelmed my sink, I felt my productivity spiral. I started falling behind on projects and my inbox with 99+ unread emails was an accurate representation of my overflowing mind. My feelings, motivation, focus, and general mood was inexplicably linked to the environment I was working in. This can be explained in a myriad of ways, but the one that resonated most for me was energy.

Energy collects in your space much like dog hair does on the stairs. Were you a kid who rearranged your room every few months when life started to feel a little blah? That's one way we shake up that stale energy, and it's one of the reasons why a clean space helps us feel more productive versus a cluttered space.

If your car is cluttered with fast-food wrappers and running on empty with the CHECK ENGINE light on, you're not going to enjoy the road trip. But when that new-car smell hits your nose, you look down at the vacuum lines in the floor mats, and you crank up your favorite playlist—all of a sudden even rush-hour traffic feels exhilarating!

After all, life IS like one big road trip—we may have a specific destination in mind or maybe we just want to take a joy ride to clear our heads. Sometimes we encounter roadblocks along the way or have to divert; some days life feels like a scenic drive, and others it feels like gridlock. While we can't always control the path we drive, we CAN control the environment in the car. With Mundane Magic, your reactions, intentions, and experience of daily life is all in your control.

When we recognize that the stuff in our space holds energy, we can see cleaning a space as a deliberate clearing of that energy, aligning the fresh energy with our specific intention. In essence, that's what we are doing here. Whether you want to feel more focused, peaceful, happy, or abundant, Mundane Magic empowers you to set the tone for your environment and thus set the tone for your life.

What Mundane Magic is not

This isn't a typical self-help book aimed to push you through resistance and discomfort. Actually, it's the opposite. Mundane Magic is meant to be easy, fun, and lighthearted. If a household task STILL feels daunting, skip it and do something that feels easier. Get a win under your belt with something simple and doable to build momentum before approaching the tigers on your to-do list. To continue the car metaphor, you wouldn't get your driving permit and then immediately go out and drive a school bus jam-packed with over-caffeinated middle schoolers the day before summer break. You'd start with something much less daunting and MAYBE work up to the chaos. Or maybe you'll decide to scratch "school bus driver" off your to-do list for good, and that's okay, too!

Speaking of to-do lists, Mundane Magic isn't meant to add to that list—we're not creating big, elaborate rituals here that'll take you all day to complete. Instead, we're incrementally adding in pockets of Magic, fun, and intention throughout your day. It can be as easy as taking three deep breaths while you make your morning coffee, then stirring a symbol with your spoon to align with your intention for the day. Mundane Magic is about taking what you already have to do and adding in what you want to do. That's novelty!

Mundane Magic also isn't a book full of motivational platitudes and one-size-fits-all advice. This book is closer to a recipe book than a self-help book, with specific ideas and directions to get you out of a rut. That said, consider everything you read within these pages as options—adapt as you see fit, substitute ingredients for what you have on hand, merge two ideas together, or do whatever feels most Magical to YOU. If your brain gets inspired to do something completely outside of the realm of this book—do that! If it feels Magical to you, run with it. If it feels more daunting, skip it. Explore this book with curiosity—there's no judgment here, because **there's no right way to create Magic in your life.**

Finally, this book isn't designed to simply make you "more productive." Mundane Magic isn't about producing more, doing more, becoming more efficient, or whatever else the self-help industry and capitalism have made us believe. **Rather than hustling through your day at the expense of creativity and joy, Mundane Magic emphasizes rest, wonder, and—most importantly—doing what works for you.** These practices aren't about doing the most; they're about doing what you *can* with reverence, while supporting your mind and body in the process. The advice in this book is about getting your mind, body, and spirit together while you clean your toilet rather than becoming the most efficient toilet cleaner on the block.

How to Use This Book

This book is structured by the spaces in the home where you're likely to have chores or routines that you're avoiding or procrastinating on. Note that you may not have all these rooms in your home (for instance, you may not have a room dedicated to laundry), and that's okay! You can use the table of contents or the index at the back of the book to find the room or chore you are looking for.

In general, each chapter categorizes tasks into three sections:

- *Daily Rituals:* These are your everyday tasks and personal care to-dos turned into small daily acts of Magic.
- *Magical Upkeep:* These are tasks you do every few days or weekly that keep your household flowing with ease and Magic.
- *Deep Magic:* These are less frequent tasks, done monthly or quarterly, that transform the energy of your home and space.

With the exception of Chapter 9, each thematic chapter will begin with Daily Rituals. I strongly encourage you to tend to your basic needs and personal care tasks before even considering moving forward to the rest of the tasks. You can even do the Daily Rituals in all the chapters before moving on to the Magical Upkeep and Deep Magic!

Why start with personal care?

Some days, the energy needed to wash your hair or plan a meal is just not there. In case no one has told you this today, you don't have to feel ashamed about it. There are plenty of reasons why you may be avoiding these tasks—it involves a lot of steps; the idea of getting out of your warm bed into the cold bathroom sucks—but maybe you simply got distracted and forgot to do it. Making your personal care tasks more Magical can help you overcome these obstacles, create a more consistent hygiene routine, and help your energy feel clearer at the same time!

We begin with personal care because it's the foundation of everything. As Abraham Maslow's hierarchy of needs shows, when your basic needs aren't met, you cannot reach self-actualization. When you haven't had lunch, you can't focus on paying your taxes. When you need to pee, you can't fold your laundry. When you're not sleeping, you won't be able to keep your kitchen tidy. Therefore, **your personal care tasks need to be the foundation of your Magical practice.** Additionally, when we neglect personal tasks, the cycle of feeling unmotivated or overwhelmed grows due to that stale energy sticking around.

Ultimately, your body holds energy from everyone and everything you encounter. This is called *transference*. You know those reusable lint rollers, the ones you can rinse off? That's kind of how your energy works. You collect energy all day long like lint on those sticky rollers, and we need to remove that energy in order to avoid getting clogged up. This can show up as tension in the body, brain fog, not sleeping well, or maybe just a sense of, to use a technical term, *blahhhhh*.

Your personal care tasks are also energy-cleansing tasks. Think of each of these Daily Rituals less like a chore and more like an opportunity to rinse the lint roller clean, to clear your energetic field so you have more energy for what you actually WANT to do today. Tend to your basic needs, and just as a fertilized garden bed grows stronger plants, watch your Magical life bloom!

> "I was really struggling at the start of the year going through a divorce. After moving out, I was forced to change up my usual daily routine: I'm only making eggs for one now, making my own coffee, and sitting down in this different office to work (I work from home). Mundane Magic tips such as stirring intention into my coffee for focus and cooking with intention have helped me to build a new routine and make my days a bit easier to get through."
>
> —Vanessa

To use this book:

1. Decide where in your home you want to begin. I recommend choosing the least overwhelming space or the most *exciting* space rather than jumping into the thing you dread the most.

    - Want to learn how to make a simmer pot for creativity or whip together a coffee spell for abundance to motivate yourself to do the dishes? Check out Chapter 5 on kitchen tasks.

- Need a burst of energy to fold your laundry or a Magic spell to find those pesky missing socks? Flip to Chapter 4 on laundry tips.
- Need motivation to organize the chaos under your bed? Open up Chapter 7 for Magical tips in the bedroom.

2. Flip to the chapter or find the chore you want to do via the index.

3. Aside from Chapter 9 and the appendix, each thematic chapter is structured into Daily Rituals, Magical Upkeep, and Deep Magic. I recommend starting in the Daily Rituals section before moving on to Magical Upkeep, and diving into Deep Magic once you feel called. You can skip around within each section if you desire, or do them in order as they are written. You do not need to complete every task in the section before moving on.

4. Review the ingredients required. In Chapter 2, I will share with you a detailed explanation of each ingredient, how to make them (if necessary), and things to consider when choosing them.

5. If the Mundane Magic spell requires an intention, decide what energy you'd like to create for this space.

6. Finally, let the instructions inspire you—feel free to make them your own and go off script. Remember that *you* are the Magic, so if your intuition or curiosity leads you to explore alternative ingredients, intentions, or ideas, go with that!

Chapter 1

Why Mundane Magic Works

How exactly is Mundane Magic going to get you to actually clean your house? It works with your brain's wiring and overcomes executive dysfunction by injecting boring tasks with a sense of novelty and fun. To begin, you need to understand the concept of Mundane Magic and why lowering the bar on your spiritual practice helps you experience more Magic in your life AND makes it easier to do the daily tasks you've been avoiding.

We create Mundane Magic by living and breathing three important maxims:

Two minutes a day is more effective than sixty minutes once a month.

How you do anything is how you do everything.

And

You are the Magic.

Ultimately, the goal of a Magical practice is to reduce the stress of daily life, not add to it. As a squiggly-brained person who struggles to keep up with ANY habit, these are maxims that I've lived by and taught to thousands of students around the world to ensure your Magical practice works FOR YOU, rather than against you.

We often think of Magic as involving big, elaborate rituals. But this puts a lot of pressure on the aesthetic of our spells, to the point where they can feel performative. At first, these rituals may feel exciting, but over time the charm wears off, especially for us neurodivergent folks. By lowering the bar on your Magical practice, you release the need to perform and instead connect deeper with yourself and your own needs. At the same time, this allows you to build a habit that serves you, rather than making Magic another thing to avoid on your to-do list.

Let's dissect each of these maxims:

Maxim #1: Two minutes a day is more effective than sixty minutes once a month.

When it comes to a Magical practice, many of us have this assumption that more is more, but I'm here to argue the opposite. Often practitioners get stuck in this cycle: life gets busy and they forget to reach for their Magic, so they feel like they've let themselves down and they decide to get back on the horse by doing a big, elaborate ritual. The problem with this all-or-nothing approach is what gets people into this cycle in the first place. When our practice requires time, energy, motivation, and fancy tools, we tend to divest ourselves from it when life gets stressful. But the fact is, the fuller your plate is, the more you need your Magical practice to support your life. I'm willing to bet your goal for your Magical practice isn't to stress yourself out, so why make your practice one more thing on your already overflowing to-do list?

2 minutes
A DAY IS
MORE
EFFECTIVE
than
60 minutes
ONCE A MONTH

The truth is, less is more when it comes to Magic. When you lower the bar on your Magical practice, you develop a sustainable practice that will truly lead to the results you're looking for.

> "The reminder about two minutes daily versus sixty minutes once a month has literally changed everything for me. It's been the difference between building a sustainable, growing practice and having Magic be another interest that doesn't see any follow-through. Keeping it simple and focusing on intentions, no matter what, has opened my mind, encouraged my imagination, and felt soooo empowering. I feel like I have permission to not be perfect and yet I know I can't mess it up—I can use what I have and still create effective spells, I don't have to choose between mundane responsibilities and exploring Magic. You foster the most brilliant blend and balance of both."
>
> —Rebecca Y.

To understand this maxim, you need to understand how your brain actually works, specifically when it comes to nervous system regulation, neural pathways, and how we form habits. When I worked with survivors of sexual violence, I was deeply entrenched in studying how the nervous system responds to stress. It was not only a part of our mandatory curriculum as advocates, but it also became a passion project for me—I'd sign up for every conference and training I could find related to it. I spent my free time listening to neuroscience podcasts and reading books about the science behind mindfulness. Understanding the wiring of your nervous system is imperative to understanding Magic—and regulating the nervous system IS the whole goal of a spiritual practice. So let's geek out about the nervous system first . . .

You have two sides to your nervous system: your sympathetic

nervous system, which is your fight/flight/freeze response, or the stress response; and your parasympathetic nervous system, which is your rest/restore/heal response, or the relaxation response. This wiring is left over from our ancestors who were running from saber-toothed tigers all day long.

When your sympathetic nervous system is activated, all your resources go toward keeping you alive: Your memory, concentration, focus are all impaired. Your pain receptors are affected, leading to more pain, tension, and inflammation in the body. Your digestion slows down, your mouth creates less saliva, so it becomes harder to break down food. Your heart rate quickens and your breath gets shallow, moving within your chest rather than your diaphragm.

Often referred to as the *fight-or-flight* response, this side of your nervous system also has a lesser-known reaction, called *freeze* (or *tonic immobility,* if you wanna get fancy!). Essentially, your brain, when faced with a "tiger," quickly assesses the best course of action for survival: You can fight the tiger off, option one. If that doesn't feel safe, you can flee or run away, option two. If running isn't an option, or if our system gets overwhelmed, we then fall into the freeze response, option three. This comes from the evolutionary survival instinct of playing dead—essentially, doing nothing, pretending to be a rotten corpse that will make the tiger sick in hopes that it will move on to fresher prey.

This freeze response shows up more often than you'd expect—think of the last time you watched a scary movie and a creature popped out and you GASPED and were frozen in your seat! That's your freeze response. Or if you've ever found yourself driving on ice and start skidding and can't think clearly enough to steer or pump the brakes so you just do nothing and gaze wide-eyed out the windshield. Maybe you remember being called to the principal's office because you rolled a snowball at recess and it hit Timmy in the head (even though Timmy was being a little jerk) and when asked what happened you just sat there like a deer in the headlights. Yep, the deer in the headlights is literally a deer assuming your headlights are a tiger and experiencing that freeze response as a result!

The thing is, though, your cute little brain doesn't know the difference between spilling your morning coffee all over your lucky shirt before a big job interview or first date and a tiger chasing you—it responds as if you were being chased by a tiger regardless. Our sympathetic nervous system gets a lot of blame because if it stays active TOO long, it creates all kinds of issues for us: chronic pain, immune system dysfunction, digestive issues, etc. Now, most of us LIVE in tiger mode all damn day—think of all the things that have already stressed you out between waking up and right now. And it's up to you to reassure your brain that you're actually okay, lest you shift into that sympathetic response. But the sympathetic nervous system isn't the enemy here—we NEED it. It's the reason you're not eating Tide Pods or walking in front of trains. It's also the reason you feel motivated to chase your goals. However, it was designed for short-term activation. A tiger is chasing you, you fight, run, or freeze, and once you're safe again, you shake it off and go back to relaxation. THAT is what you were wired to do. Most of us struggle to get out of that tiger mode once it's activated.

Now, here's a fun fact: there's a ninety-second chemical reaction in your brain beginning when you experience stress. What you do in those ninety seconds MATTERS. It determines whether you stay in that sympathetic state or go back into parasympathetic mode, where all those resources utilized for survival can go back to finding balance in the body and mind again.

Imagine this:

You're driving to work and get cut off in traffic—what is your instinctive reaction? If it is to curse the driver and slam on your horn, congratulations—you've identified your FIGHT response! That is how many of us are wired in this situation. Now, imagine you spend the next ninety seconds cursing the person and flipping them the bird. Your cute little brain (which, again, thinks that car is a LITERAL TIGER) is saying to itself, "Oh gosh, we are really upset, we are yelling and screaming, we must be fighting, which means that car MUST be an actual tiger, which means I must divert all resources to survival IMMEDIATELY." You spend the rest of your commute steaming over how no one knows how to drive anymore.

Then you get to the office and someone has taken your parking spot. GREAT—what else can go wrong today? You walk in the door and Jeremy at the front desk says, "Hey, nice shirt," and you think to yourself, *WTF, Jeremy, I wear this every week. Is he mocking me?* By the time you get to your desk, you're so upset you can't focus on the to-do list in front of you, so when your boss pops in about a project deadline that got moved up, you totally lose it.

How does THAT situation impact your day at work? Your commute home? Your time spent with friends or family after work? How does it affect your environment? Your motivation to do ANYTHING productive?

Oh, by the way, when that sympathetic nervous system response gets activated, your endocrine system pumps stress hormones like cortisol and adrenaline into your bloodstream. Those hormones can linger in your body for up to twelve hours. Meaning, if you freak out on your commute to work, you're still feeling that effect in your body on your drive home.

When you practice Magic, you start to familiarize yourself with your needs and how you're feeling moment by moment. That tiger response becomes recognizable, and with that awareness you have space to choose a different response.

Now imagine that same scenario, but you've been practicing two minutes of Mundane Magic with your daily chores. You get cut off in traffic and you recognize that instinctive fight response. But you catch yourself instead. You take a deep breath. You tell yourself, *I am safe.* You feel the support underneath your hips. You spend those ninety seconds reassuring your brain and body that you are not in danger. Your brain goes, "HUH, okay, I thought this was a tiger but I'm breathing much deeper than I would be if I was running for my life . . . It must not be a tiger after all. I must be safe." So you stay in that parasympathetic (relaxation) response.

You get to work and someone has taken your parking spot, but you smile because it's a nice day to take a longer walk into the office. Jeremy compliments your shirt and you say, "Thank you!" You sit down at your desk and can mentally plan out your priorities, so when your boss moves up a deadline, you feel like you have space to tackle it.

How did that ninety-second reaction alter your day at work? Your commute home? Your time spent with friends or family after work? How does it affect your environment? Which scenario would you feel more productive in?

THIS is Mundane Magic. When you practice the tools laid out for you in this book, **you're practicing micro moments of mindfulness, of centering, of coming back to yourself.** After all, that's what all Magical practices are based on. All these tools allow you to better recognize the reactions of your nervous system and reassure your cute little brain that there's no tiger here.

A lot of people think they need to do big, elaborate rituals in order to be a "real witch" or in order to see "real results," but I disagree. **Ultimately, when it comes to your nervous system, consistency is more important than duration.** If you only practiced a big, elaborate, sixty-minute ritual occasionally, you might feel great afterward, but it won't have the same lasting impact on your daily life and your nervous system.

By practicing these micro moments of nervous system regulation when you're folding laundry or brushing your teeth, new neural pathways are created in your brain that allow you to actually access the parasympathetic nervous system when stress pops up in your everyday life. THAT is how we find Magic in the mundane.

Time and time again, I have seen my students experience greater results in their life by adding small doses of Magic into their preexisting routines. Called *habit stacking,* it's a powerful tool for actually sticking with your spiritual practice. (For clarity, I'll be using the terms *Magical practice* and *spiritual practice* interchangeably; you should use whatever words resonate most with your practice!)

Mundane Magic both capitalizes on your preexisting habits by making them more Magical AND allows you to ritualize the habits you WANT to create by infusing them with novelty and mindfulness. If you have a neurodivergent/squiggly brain like mine, you know that sticking to things is even harder for us. Your brain CRAVES novelty, something to make brushing your teeth more interesting so your brain allows you to focus on it. We can use Magic to overcome the executive dysfunction that prevents us from starting a task.

Maxim #2: How you do anything is how you do everything.

> "As an introvert teacher, I find the noise and business of school to be very draining. Through Mundane Magic I have learned how to pay attention to my energy levels. Which has helped me save my energy for my students instead of getting bogged down in all the rest of the responsibilities."
>
> —Karla S.

I'm willing to bet that if I asked you what your goal for a Magical practice is, you would NOT say, "To stress myself out." My guess is, you want your spiritual practice to reduce stress in your life, or at the very least make the inevitable stress of life more manageable. If that's the goal, then why do we put so much pressure on our spirituality

HOW YOU DO

Anything

IS HOW YOU DO

Everything

that it becomes one more thing on our to-do list to stress us out? When you inevitably keep putting your practice off, consistency will evade you.

First, if this is you, you're not alone. There are so many reasons WHY we do this—namely because we live in a capitalist society that benefits from our feeling like we're never doing "enough" and that simple or easy is ineffective. Magic is an undoing of this wiring. My belief is that your spiritual practice is a journey home to your true self beneath the beliefs that have been programmed into you about what you "should" be doing. **Your true self is a home of joy, contentment, self-love, and compassion. It isn't a productivity machine; it's a rest machine.**

If that is the journey we are taking, the actual destination isn't nearly as important as the path we take. If your spiritual practice is a big, elaborate hoopla every single time, that reinforces this wiring that you're never good enough on your own. So what's the answer?

Lower the bar. All the way to the floor.

Let the bar for your practice be so low you can trip over it on your worst days.

How you do anything is how you do everything means that:

- When you cut yourself some slack, you're more able to tap into the self-love that's dormant within you.
- When you let your practice come intuitively and infuse into your daily life, your intuition starts to grow stronger.
- When your spiritual practice becomes more about doing less than it is about doing more, you give a big old energetic middle finger to capitalism.

- When you allow your spiritual practice to be FUN and lighthearted, you experience more fun and lightheartedness in your life.

After all, you're not practicing Magic to get really good at Magic . . . You're practicing to get better at life.

Maxim #3: You are the Magic.

"Simple tasks like making a cup of tea have become a ritual to me that I treasure."

—Kristen J.

If you're new to Magic, you are probably worried about doing it "right." Maybe you got a little nervous earlier when I said you can color outside the lines and go off script when exploring this book. Again, this is that capitalistic wiring talking—we are raised to look outside ourselves for the answers. Of course, there are times when this is necessary, like going to a licensed doctor when we are really sick. But, unfortunately, more and more our society has started to reinforce this false belief that everything we need is external.

This always reminds me of the psychological principle of *intrinsic* versus *extrinsic* motivation. Stay with me here while we geek out about the brain again . . .

Intrinsic motivation is within you—I want to crochet a hat because I enjoy the act of crocheting; it makes me feel happy. Extrinsic motivation is outside of you—I want to crochet a hat because I want to sell it or post about it on social media or crochet more than my neighbor Adrien. While both intrinsic and extrinsic motivations have value, when you initially begin with intrinsic motivation (I like this thing; it makes me happy) and you suddenly apply extrinsic motivation (I do this thing to make money, receive rewards, etc.),

You
ARE THE
Magic

you then lose that intrinsic motivation. I saw this firsthand when I decided I wanted to pursue acting as a career in college.

I was practically born onstage—growing up, I was always running from rehearsal to rehearsal. But when grades, accolades, and career opportunities suddenly came into the mix, I started to resent acting. I stopped auditioning and enjoying the thrill of an opening night performance. If you've ever turned a passion into a career, you might be nodding your head at this.

This is so dangerous because extrinsic motivation is fleeting. You have no control over what happens outside of you. You can crochet a beautiful hat that you're super proud of and still not sell it at the craft market. **When we rely on extrinsic motivators alone, we're placing a gamble on our motivation—and as with all gambling, we often lose.**

Intrinsic motivation, however, is self-sustaining. It's one hundred percent in your control. If you love the thing, do the thing. If it feels new and novel, you're more likely to do it. If you experience joy, contentment, and fun from doing something, you don't need to bend over backward to make time for it. Now, even if you LOVE the thing, it can be hard to get started—even the most passionate guitar players sometimes struggle to pick up their instrument. So that's where infusing novelty into our tasks comes into play!

You are the Magic is like a pilot light to stay guided by intrinsic motivation. YOU are the Magic and the special ingredient that makes anything in this book work. This book can collect dust on your shelf, or it can change the way you look at your boring daily tasks. What's the difference between those options? Not me, not what's written on this page, but YOU. You decide to keep reading, you decide to experiment, you decide to be intentional about the things you do daily. It doesn't work without you.

When it comes to Magic in general, your intention is the fuel. How you place your focus on the spell changes its results. We'll talk more about intention in the next chapter, but I want you to lean in and hear this again:

Magic doesn't work without you. Let your intrinsic motivators—aka your joy of the ritual, your excitement over the novelty, your curiosity and exploration—be your guide throughout this journey.

Oh, and remember that second maxim? When you're guided by intrinsic motivators in your Magical practice, you'll notice you do so in other areas of your life, too. You might just find the motivation you've been missing was underneath the surface of extrinsic factors all along!

Motivation and Overcoming Obstacles

So obviously the next step is making that practice *actually happen*. Now that you have the basic tenets, let's tackle the reason you haven't gotten started yet: your motivation. Specifically, how do you get back to that intrinsic motivation so you can create sustainable change in your life?

Motivation fluctuates for a number of reasons, but chances are if you feel totally stuck it's because you've hit one of these three obstacles:

1. I don't have time.
2. I don't have the energy.
3. I don't know where to start.

We'll tackle each together—*Magically,* of course!

"I don't have time."

As a way to overcome this excuse, you've probably heard the millennial adage "You have the same number of hours in a day as

Beyoncé." But honestly, that's bullshit. Beyoncé has a team of people, cash, and privilege that allow her to do it all. So instead of comparing yourself to a superstar, why not give yourself permission to do what is within your means?

The two-minutes-a-day rule applies not only to spirituality, but also to the tasks you're avoiding. What would help your hydration more—chugging a giant gallon of water at once or sipping a glass of water every few hours? What will help your body become more active—running a marathon with zero preparation or taking a walk around the block a few times a day? What will help your kitchen become more functional—doing a giant deep clean only once a week or picking up two dishes after each meal throughout the day?

If you have two minutes, you have time to do this! I know you KNOW this logically, but if you're still struggling to get started it's likely because of the next obstacle.

"I don't have the energy."

I get it—when your to-do list is a mile long, it can feel like a bear to even get started. Now add on top of that the stress of work, family, and late-stage capitalism. Double that if you experience chronic pain, fatigue, or are neurodivergent. **You're allowed to feel tired AND you're also allowed to rest.** Give yourself that permission, again, to not have to do it all. You're not Beyoncé; you're *human.*

The purpose of this book isn't to give you superpowers so you can tackle your entire to-do list in an hour or deep clean your whole house in a day. The purpose is to give you permission to cut yourself some slack—to make those day-to-day tasks that you KNOW will help you feel better a little easier so you can preserve the energy you have. But we need to tackle one more obstacle before we dive in . . .

"I don't know where to start."

Have you ever heard the advice to "eat the frog"—aka tackle the most stressful thing on your to-do list first? Yeah, throw it out the window. Give yourself permission to start with the EASIEST task on your list instead so you can actually build momentum rather than burning out hot and fast. This book is organized based on spaces in your home—to get started, decide which area of your home feels the LEAST overwhelming to tackle and flip to that section to begin. Once you finish that space, move on to the next space that feels easy to tackle, and so on until you reach the rooms that feel more difficult. By that point, you'll have the momentum you need to tackle those more challenging spaces and chores.

If you don't have a multiple-room space (for instance, if you live in a dorm or studio apartment), start with the easiest task on your to-do list and find that in the appropriate section of the book. Go from task to task until you have the momentum you need to continue.

Now that you know WHERE to start, it's time to get your butt in gear. Next, we'll talk about what you'll need to start (hint: it's way simpler than you think!). But first, if two minutes is all you have energy for, here's something you can do right NOW that will boost your energy and motivate you to get started.

Motivation Simmer Pot Recipe

INGREDIENTS:

- **Water** *(enough to fill three-quarters of your pot—the size doesn't matter!)*
- **Oranges** *or* **orange juice** *to energize and add joy (a few slices or a splash will do!)*
- **A dash of dried mint** *for clarity and energy*
- **A few apple slices** *to cut yourself some slack*
- **A pinch of salt** *for protection*

INSTRUCTIONS:

- Place all the ingredients in a pot on the stove and set the burner to high.
- Once the water starts bubbling, drop it to a simmer and set a timer to check on it every fifteen minutes.
- Continue to add water as needed. The ingredients do not need to be completely submerged; just do not let the water completely dry out.
- While the simmer pot bubbles on the stove, it will infuse your space with scent and intention.
- Use this time to create some momentum and crack open this book to the section where you feel most called to begin.

Chapter 2

Tools for Getting Started

Grab your sticky notes, friend, because you're going to be flipping back to this section often throughout your journey with Mundane Magic. You're about to discover the ingredients needed to make ANY chore more Magical, from intention setting to the basic practices and ingredients you'll need to incorporate the tips shared in the rest of the book. And if you're feeling unmotivated and overwhelmed, don't fret: at the end of this chapter we'll use Magic to overcome common roadblocks to completing the tasks laid out in the book in ways that will energize even the most lethargic witches.

A quick note before we dive in: Your Magical practices need to work for YOU and YOUR belief systems. **See the contents of this book as inspiration, not prescription.** If something doesn't resonate—skip it! If your belief system says something different, adjust as you need to! You are in the driver's seat here when it comes to turning your daily life into a Magical experience, and you really can't screw it up when following your intuition.

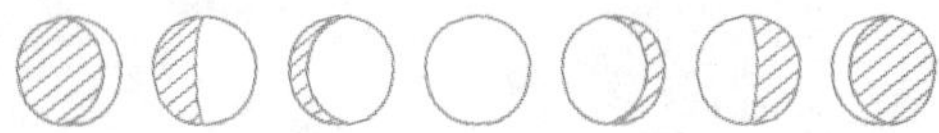

Ritualizing Your Routines

When was the last time you washed your shower curtain liner? I bet you can't give me a specific date. In fact, I'm willing to bet you throw out a fair number of shower curtain liners each year because mold and mildew build up on them. I know you do because I did this, too. I had my favorite shower curtain on auto-delivery every three months because I was so bad about washing it. Until I started ritualizing my chores.

One of the biggest roadblocks to actually doing chores is remembering when they need to get done. Take your shower curtain liner. It gets gross because you can't remember the last time you washed it until it's visibly icky, and by that point it's too late. Think about how that impacts you every time you shower—you look down and think, *URGH, what is that pink-and-black stuff growing near my legs?*

A lot of us feel a sense of shame when this happens, like, *Why did I let it go this long?* But the truth is, you have so much to keep track of in your brain every day that your shower curtain liner is not even a blip on the radar, nor should it be. So instead of trying to remember when you last did every single chore in your space, ritualizing these tasks makes remembering them automatic.

Enter the lunar cycle.

Maybe you've heard of this cute little rock floating around us called "the moon." It tends to move in phases from new moon to full moon and back again. The moon and Magic go hand in hand. We often ritualize the new and full moon anyway—so why not feed two worms with one apple and get those pesky chores done while aligning with the moon's energy?

> "One of my biggest uses [for the lunar cycle] is using moon phase and season to remind me of chores. So at the full moon, I do a full bed cleanse, rotate mattress, wash mattress cover, etc. Sheets get changed at new moon. Each season change it's time to deep clean certain things. It takes the 'When did I do this last?' out of the equation and I feel less compelled to be like, *Ugh I don't wanna*. I just do it because it's time to do it and it feels like it helps with overall energy."
>
> —Nikki B.

New moon chores

The new moon is traditionally connected to the energy of manifesting, creating, or calling in what you want to make manifest in the next lunar cycle. It's the time when the moon is least visible, so there is the most space to welcome new energy into your life.

To welcome this energy in, **you need space** to accept new things into your life. If you're trying to manifest new friendships but your schedule is already jam-packed, how can you possibly have space to get to know someone new? Aligning with the new moon's energy means allowing that space in your physical environment AND your schedule. Now, does this mean I can't water my plants outside of the new moon? Of course not. But if creating structure in your routine helps you, you can use the new moon as an opportunity to build structure, novelty, and Magic into those routine tasks that often fall through the cracks.

In addition to space, **you need a plan**: How are you going to bring this thing into your life? What are you creating space for? What will you do when it shows up? The new moon's energy is asking you to get organized and to get clear on what you want to invite in.

And finally, **you need to take action**. Manifestation isn't just asking the moon for what you want; it's putting in the work to get that thing. If you want to make new friends, you need to get out and meet new people, you need to schedule get-togethers, you need to put yourself out there and DM that person you think is cool. The new moon is all about setting the scene so you can follow through the rest of the month.

Now think about the chores you do at home that help you create space, plan, and take action. These could include organizing the spice cabinet, mapping out your paid time off for the next month, finally making that doctor's appointment, or creating a budget for yourself. When you do chores like these during the new moon phase, you automatically start to align with this energy. And because how you do anything is how you do everything, you start to notice your manifestations coming to you FASTER!

Some new moon chore ideas are:

- Meal prepping to help you plan and act on your health goals
- Watering and fertilizing your houseplants to represent your own growth
- Organizing the fridge or pantry to make space for new ingredients

- Making a doctor's appointment (the one you've been putting off!) to clear space in your brain for other fun things
- Budgeting to plan to grow your abundance

Use the following chart as inspiration to create your own New Moon Chore Chart. As you move through this book, you'll find suggestions for which chores may best fit the new moon. If you want to create a chore chart for yourself to follow each month, you'll find a blank template in the appendix at the back of the book (page 277).

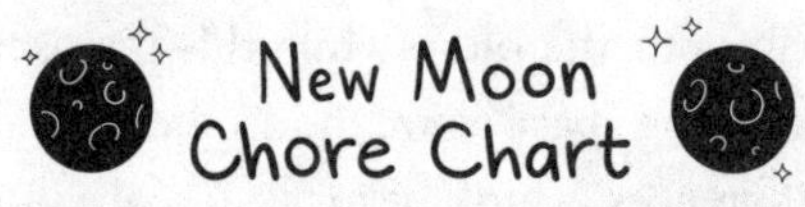

Water or fertilize plants	Organize the fridge	Clear out the freezer and pantry
Make doctors' appointments	Create space in your calendar for self-care	Declutter your closet
Rearrange the furniture	Refill prescriptions	Budgeting

Full moon chores

On the other side of your new moon rituals are your full moon rituals. The full moon is often associated with cleansing and release. Think about how, if you have a full plate at a buffet, you don't have any room for dessert. You need to remove something to make room for something new. When the moon is full, it is the most visible in the sky, so it can illuminate the things you need to release in your life. Think about when the sun streams in and illuminates the dust on your TV console. The light makes you aware of it, so you can no longer ignore it until it's taken care of.

When it comes to manifestation, you have to release the old to welcome in the new. If you want to grow your business, you must **release** the fear that your friends will think you're weird for posting about it on Instagram. If you want to be a public speaker, you have to **release** the fear of public speaking. If you want to stock up on fresh groceries, you have to **clean out** the old moldy grapes taking up space in the back of your fridge.

Now think about the chores at home that assist with this release and clearing out the old—while this may sound similar to the process of making space as we did in the new moon, there are some subtle differences. Think of making space in the new moon as broadening the space that is already present, like adding some flexibility to your calendar for that birthday party or career opportunity, while the clearing and releasing for the full moon involves removing things that take up space unnecessarily—think decluttering, deep cleaning, those pesky cleaning tasks that don't need to be done every week but probably should be done at least once a month. Cleaning the baseboards, vacuuming under the couch, decluttering your wallet or purse. When you start syncing these chores with the full moon, you'll notice the energy in your space feels lighter and clearer. AND you'll never forget when you last washed your shower curtain again!

Use the following chart as inspiration to create your own Full Moon Chore Chart. You'll find a blank template in the appendix at the back of the book (page 277).

Solstice/equinox chores

Now I know what you're thinking: *Molly, what about those tasks that need to be done LESS than once a month? How can I make those*

Wash the duvet	Change the shower curtain liner	Vacuum under the couch
Clean the baseboards	Wash the car	Dust on top of the fridge
Clean out your wallet or purse	Take an everything shower	Pay any outstanding bills

Magical? The answer is in the seasonal shifts, the solstices and equinoxes. These happen every three months, so they are perfect for clearing out stagnant energy and recommitting to your intentions. While similar to the clearing we did for the full moon, these are great opportunities for Deep Magic that doesn't get done as often. Think "fresh start" vibes—what tasks help you feel brand-new?

While the dates change year to year for these seasonal shifts, here's a general guideline of when they occur—note that these dates are for the Northern Hemisphere; go ahead and flip-flop them if you live in the Southern Hemisphere:

- Spring equinox: March 19, 20, or 21
- Summer solstice: June 20, 21, or 22
- Autumn equinox: September 22 or 23
- Winter solstice: December 20, 21, or 22

Use the following chart as inspiration to create your own Solstice/Equinox Chore Chart. You'll find a blank template in the appendix at the back of the book (page 278). As you create your seasonal chore chart, decide which tasks you need to get done on a quarterly basis. You could make one chart for the entire year, filled with tasks that need to get done repeatedly. Or you could make a new chart each season and add some tasks that only need to get done once per year.

Solstice/Equinox Chore Chart

Change your toothbrush	Rearrange or redecorate a room	Donate clothes that don't fit anymore
Purge phone contacts	Clean the oven	Vacuum under the fridge
Deep clean the dryer vents	Degrease the outdoor grill	Get your car's oil changed

Ingredients for Getting Started

Throughout this book, you'll be introduced to new ways to add Magic to everyday chores, tasks, and projects. Each section will reference ingredients needed to complete the task. To keep things simple, I'll be explaining each ingredient here so you can easily flip back and forth while reading.

Intention

Intention is perhaps the most important ingredient in this entire book. If you add only intention to your daily tasks, you will make them Magical. You don't need fifty-seven thousand crystals or even a fancy affirmation. You can simply hold your intention in your awareness while you clean your toilet, and it will become a Magical ritual. Remember, *you* are the Magic!

Now, don't overthink this. A lot of people wonder if their intentions are "right" or how exactly to word their intention. Let's begin the same way the word does, with *intent.* Intent means you have a purpose for what you are doing, a determination, and an eager attention. So, when forming an intention, we need **purpose, determination,** and **attention**. Notice what's missing here. We don't need a fancy incantation that rhymes, grammatically correct sentence structure, or even a perfectly focused mind. **If you are determined to do something on purpose and give attention to it, you are setting an intention.**

Think to yourself right now: Why are you reading this book? What is the purpose? What do you want to achieve? Where is your attention while your eyes scan this page? The answers do not need to be complicated. Maybe you're doing some light reading before bed or someone gave you the book as a gift and you feel rude not reading it. Either way, you have an intention to continue on to the next sentence.

When we're making Magic, we're using intention. That is the key ingredient. Rosemary is great for cleansing and protecting energy. Now, you can eat rosemary focaccia all the livelong day, but unless you decide that you are consuming it with the intention of cleansing and protecting your energy, you're just getting full on bread. (Which, honestly, also sounds great!)

Why is intention SO important in Magic? Because YOU—not the ingredients you're using—are the Magic. In the example above, the rosemary isn't activated until you set your intention. When it comes to how our brains work, this is also true.

If I asked you, "Hey, reader, how many gray Prius cars did you see today?" I guarantee you wouldn't be able to answer. But if I said, "Hey, reader, set the intention to count how many gray Prius cars you pass today," you'd start seeing them EVERYWHERE. There's not Magically MORE of this car on the road; it's because your brain is now focused on them.

This is the reticular activating system (RAS) of your brain at work. Think of the RAS like a filtration system: it's taking in all the cars you pass at any given moment, but you're not consciously aware of every single make and model because you simply don't need to archive that information. Your conscious brain can only process so much information at one time; in fact, research shows you receive anywhere from eleven million bits to over a billion bits of information at any given second while your conscious brain can only process between ten and fifty of those bits. So your RAS makes a lot of choices about what you process consciously. That's why when you set an intention to count gray Prius cars, you see more of them. Your RAS is clocking that car and pulling it through the filter to your conscious mind.

Relating this to Magic is incredibly powerful. If you start doing abundance rituals, your RAS will pick up on more small examples of abundance in your day-to-day life. If you take a self-love ritual bath, your RAS will start filtering more loving thoughts to your conscious mind.

That is why YOU are the Magic, and your intention is the fuel that proves this to you. This is why every single Magical spell, in this book or otherwise, requires an intention. Because this is a given going forward, I won't be listing "intention" as an ingredient for every spell here, but I will be offering example intentions for certain chores to get your wheels turning as you formulate your own intentions.

Affirmations

Affirmations are short, positive statements that reflect your intentions. You'll find a few affirmation examples in the following chart or you can choose to make your own.

A good rule of thumb for affirmations is that

they should be written in the positive and present tense as opposed to negative intentions that are framed in the future tense. In general, present tense affirmations will begin with the words "I am," "I have," or "I feel." Here's a look at the difference:

NEGATIVE, FUTURE TENSE	POSITIVE, PRESENT TENSE
I won't be stressed	I am relaxed
I'll stop being mean to myself	I am kind to myself
I'll get rid of my debts	I have more than enough to pay these debts

Affirmations and intentions go hand in hand. Think of your intention first, then list a few affirmations that describe what it would be like, right here and now, if that intention were already true.

Do affirmations feel hokey to you? Here we apply the "fake it till you make it" concept, which actually has a scientific basis. Did you know that smiling can reduce blood pressure, relieve stress, and even improve immune system function? When you smile, your brain sends out hormones that improve your mood. These include endorphins, which relieve pain and stress; dopamine, which makes you feel good; serotonin, which is a natural antidepressant; and neuropeptides, which help fight off stress. After all, you wouldn't be smiling if a tiger were chasing you, right?

Here's the kicker, though: it doesn't matter if you're actually smiling because you're happy or you're just turning the corners of your mouth upward. Your cute little brain can be easily tricked into feeling better even if the smile you're slapping on feels "fake." AND this creates a fun little feedback loop in your brain: I turn the corners of my mouth up into a smile, my brain releases happy hormones, I feel happy, I smile, repeat.

Affirmations are kind of like smiles—even if you feel like you're "faking it," there's some part of your body and mind that is ingesting the affirmations as if they were true. Bonus points if you say them with a smile!

Color Magic

Color Magic is perhaps the easiest tool for adding Magic into your everyday, simply by being intentional about which colors you bring into each experience. This could be when you choose your outfit for the day, or even when you paint your house or nails!

Medical students who wear white lab coats during exams do better because of the association the students have with that specific-colored coat. *White lab coat* signals to the unconscious part of their brain that they are a successful doctor, therefore giving them the confidence to do well. Remember the "fake it till you make it" principle we just talked about? Now, dye the lab coat purple and we no longer have that association, so the lab coat no longer has the same effect on the student.

Now let's think about how color impacts us at a restaurant. Did you know that fast-food chains often opt for red or yellow decor because these colors are thought to stimulate appetite? Imagine walking into a restaurant that used a lot of green in their branding—would you expect this restaurant to serve ice cream or salads? We often associate green in restaurants with health and freshness because of its association to nature.

What kind of car do you drive? Have you ever noticed what color your dashboard lights are? Often sports cars will use red lights and instruments to denote urgency and excitement. On the other hand, sedans will use blue or green lighting to promote calmness, while eco-conscious cars use these colors to reflect their environmental focus.

Pink has been used in prison cells to promote calmness and reduce aggression; stores painted with cool colors like blue or green tend to encourage customers to linger; offices paint their walls blue to promote focus—color psychology is all around us. You're already impacted by color, so why not bring your intention to it and take control of that impact?!

The most important thing is for you to have a meaningful association with the color. Below is a list of common Color Magic associations—but YOUR associations are the Magic here. Remember how in middle school you'd choose your folder color based on which color "felt" like math? This is the vibe of Color Magic. So, if red feels more like abundance to you, go with that over anything else!

COLOR	INTENTIONS
Red	Grounding, motivation
Orange	Creativity, energy
Yellow	Clarity, confidence
Green	Abundance, growth
Blue	Communication, calm
Purple	Intuition, spiritual connection
Pink	Love, self-love
Black	Protection, warding off negativity
White	Healing, any intention

Meditation

If you struggle with meditation, let me make a case for why you shouldn't close this book right now. In all likelihood, you might struggle with meditation because you:

A. Can't sit still
B. Have a squirrelly brain that can't focus
C. Are in an environment that is too loud or chaotic
D. Find it so mind-numbingly boring you avoid it

What if I told you A, B, and C aren't actually problems, and D will be solved as you read the rest of this book? Hear me out.

Meditation gets a bad rap because people think you need to sit like some swami on top of a perfectly serene mountain with an empty mind in order to do it "right." But that is actually WRONG. My first ever meditation gig was teaching at a rock climbing gym on a cement floor directly below the stairs to a kids' camp. The room had zero insulation in it, so between the techno beats, the cheering outside the door when someone hit the top of the bouldering wall, and the stampede of elephants running above us every ten minutes, you would think it was the worst possible spot for meditation. But it turned out to be the BEST space to meditate.

Meditation simply means paying attention to what is happening, while it is happening. Your brain is thinking all day long; most of those thoughts are completely unconscious (hello, eleven million bits per second), so your brain is making decisions without your input All. Day. Long. Of course your brain will get busier the moment you sit down to meditate. That's like driving seventy miles per hour on the highway and then slamming on the brakes—of course all the stuff from the backseat is going to come forward. Of course your brain is going to feel squirrelly. Of course you're going to remember the seventy-two trillion things you forgot to do. Of course you're going to start planning your grocery list.

But here's the thing—if your brain is really distracted during meditation, it's actually a sign your meditation practice is WORKING. Because all those thoughts and distractions would have happened anyway, and now you are aware of them. With that awareness, you can choose: Am I going to continue to build my grocery list, or am I going to set that aside and take a deep breath? Am I going to continue saying mean things to myself about how I suck at meditating, or am I going to set that aside and be nice to myself?

When I taught meditation at the rock climbing gym, I would invite my students to turn their awareness TOWARD the noises outside the space. Noticing their reaction to the distractions helped soften their attitude toward them, and eventually they didn't feel fazed by them at all. And because how you do anything is how you do everything, those students started to notice that they became less fazed by distractions outside the meditation space, too.

You see, if we only practice meditation in perfect conditions, it doesn't train us for real life. Every time you notice your brain wandering off in meditation, and you guide your attention back with kindness and compassion toward yourself, you're strengthening your concentration. Think of it like going to the brain gym and working on your mental muscles for focus, empathy, and emotional regulation.

You don't suck at meditation—because you CAN'T suck at meditation. And if you find it boring, just wait until you see how pairing mundane tasks with meditation somehow make both a lot LESS boring.

Spoiler alert: Anything can be meditation. Walking your dog, washing the dishes, playing Candy Crush, even reading this book can be a meditation. To meditate is as simple as focusing on what is happening with curiosity instead of leaping to judgment—that's it. When your mind wanders off to your to-do list—which it will do often, by the way—you simply notice that you are distracted and gently refocus your attention. You do this again, and again, and again . . . and again.

The goal isn't to clear the mind or quiet your thoughts so much as it is to *neutralize your reaction* to those thoughts. **Through meditation, we turn expectations into curiosity, doubt into trust, and judgment into compassion.** Remember the tiger prowling around your nervous system? When you practice meditation, you become aware of the threat your brain is focused on, and through curiosity and compassion you reassure yourself that it's not a tiger after all. Try this meditation on for size.

MEDITATION

Find Calm in Chaotic Environments

Let your eyes close or you could rest your gaze to the floor, whatever feels best for you.

Take a deep breath in, really hear the sound of your inhale, open your mouth, and audibly sigh. Do that one more time. Breathe in, then make a sound with your exhale.

A lot of times we think in order to meditate we need to be super focused and we need to be in a space that is serene and beautiful and peaceful, but that is just not the case. And so here, when you're in your imperfect conditions, just start to notice what sounds are around you.

Maybe it's the sound of your refrigerator humming, your air conditioner, your heater. Maybe you can hear traffic noises outside, your cat purring.

Just let the sounds drift in one ear and out the other. No need to make up a story around them being good or bad. No need to label them or figure out their source. Just let yourself really hear and listen.

Now bring your awareness to the most obvious sound. Whatever sounds the loudest or the most apparent comes into your ears first. Just let yourself narrow in on that sound. Really hear it. Almost like you're trying to pick out the clarinet from an orchestral performance. Really tune in to that one sound.

Now let yourself notice the most subtle sound you can pick up on. The quietest, the one you really have to pay attention to hear. Let your awareness tune in to that sound now.

Now get curious. What's the furthest sound your ears can reach? Maybe it's a sound outside the building or the room you're in. What's the sound that is furthest from you?

Let your shoulders relax as you listen.

Now tune in to sounds closer to you, sounds within the space or the room you're in. See if you can fully experience each sound.

Now bring your awareness to the closest sounds of all, the sounds within you: the sound of your breath, your stomach digesting lunch, your heartbeat. Notice any sounds within.

Once again, bring your awareness to all the sounds around you. The symphony of sounds floating in one ear and then the other. And just notice how your mind and body feel as you sit with the sounds.

Take one more deep breath in, open your mouth, and let it go.

Gratitude and Little Treat Magic

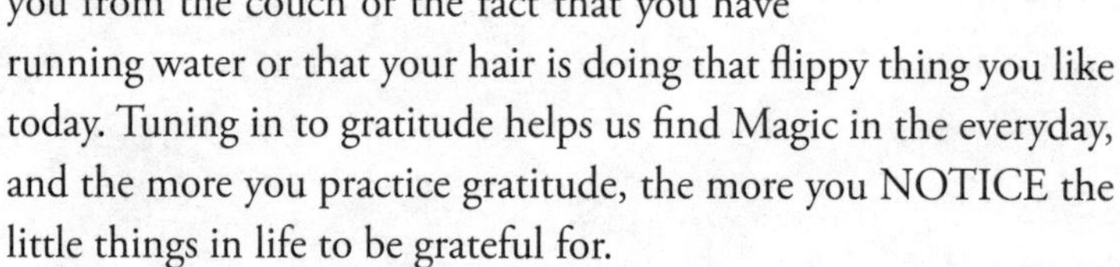

Hand in hand with meditation and intention, gratitude asks us to turn our focus toward the things we appreciate in our current experience. Maybe it's the way your dog looks up at you from the couch or the fact that you have running water or that your hair is doing that flippy thing you like today. Tuning in to gratitude helps us find Magic in the everyday, and the more you practice gratitude, the more you NOTICE the little things in life to be grateful for.

Now, we often express gratitude to others, but when was the last time you offered gratitude to yourself? You need your own gratitude just as much as, if not more than, anyone else. Gratitude is a powerful motivator to keep going—and so we can add more self-imposed gratitude into our lives by implementing Little Treat Magic.

Little Treat Magic is so simple you're probably already doing it. When you feel unmotivated or you've completed a tough task, give yourself a little treat as a token of gratitude. Think of it like when a dog sits on command: they get a treat, and you deserve one, too!

Little Treat Magic plays a role in a psychological process called *conditioning*. Perhaps you've heard of Pavlov and his dogs? Every time he rang a bell, Pavlov would feed the dogs. Eventually, the dogs became conditioned to expect food at the sound of the bell, initiating the salivary response. Even when the food was taken away, the dogs would still salivate at the sound. With Little Treat Magic, you're creating new stimulus-response connections: when I empty my inbox, I get a little treat, thus I become more motivated to empty my inbox.

The key to Little Treat Magic is in the name: it must be little—this isn't a trip to Disney World or a new car. *Little* means inexpensive and easy to obtain right NOW. *Treat* means it must feel like a treat, not a chore. For example, if you love fountain sodas, take some time out of your day to go get one! But Little Treat Magic also doesn't have to be something you eat or buy. If you want to sit on the couch and rewatch *Gossip Girl* for the eleventh time, do that. Maybe your little treat is reading a book or taking a deep breath—you get to decide for yourself!

Let your Little Treat Magic both reward your efforts around the house and inspire you to keep going—it's so simple, but that's what makes it Magic!

Sigils

Sigils are symbols you create and infuse with a specific intention. Your subconscious mind actually communicates to you through symbology—that's why your dreams have funny images in them. As humans, we respond emotionally to symbols all day long. Think about how you react to seeing the Golden Arches when you're really, really hungry. Or how you feel when you see the symbol of a hate group. Sigils are a Magical practice of creating your own symbol and emotional association to that symbol. The more you use a sigil, the stronger the association becomes, and the more powerful it is. Let's walk through how to make your own sigil:

1. Write down your intention in the positive, present tense like it is already happening. For example: *I am relaxed, I am protected, I have enough, I am worthy, I feel safe,* etc.

   Let's use "I AM PROTECTED" for our examples.

2. Now cross off any repeating letters.

   I AM PROTEC~~TE~~D

3. Skipping the crossed-off letters, use the chart below to find the number associated with each of the letters in your intention.

For our intention, the numbers are 9 1 4 7 9 6 2 5 3 4.

1	2	3	4	5	6	7	8	9
A	B	C	D	E	F	G	H	I
J	K	L	M	N	O	P	Q	R
S	T	U	V	W	X	Y	Z	

4. Cross off any duplicate numbers from your intention and rewrite your new number below:

9 1 4 7 ~~9~~ 6 2 5 3 ~~4~~

Our new number is: 9 1 4 7 6 2 5 3

5. Using the circle provided below, draw lines starting from your first number, going to the second number, and each number after. An example is provided in the accompanying image:

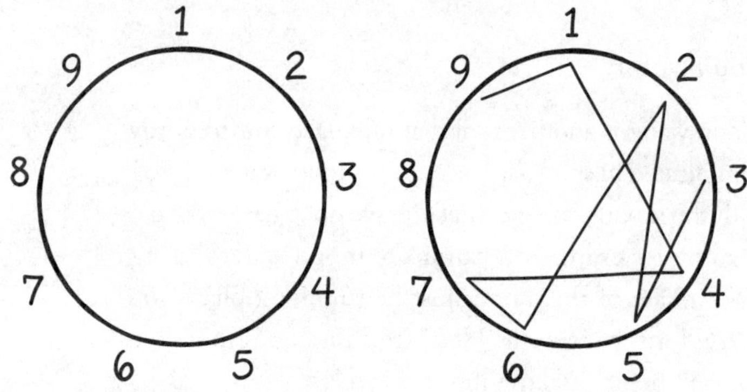

6. If you have overlapping lines, you can space them out slightly or make a really thick, bold line instead. If you end up with only one line, you can create from that! Now you have the base of your sigil. It's time to PLAY! Add your own

flourish, doodles, bits, and bobs until it looks just right! There's no way to screw this up, so have fun with it. Here's how my example sigil came out:

7. Finally, it's time to infuse your sigil with intention. Hold your original intention in your awareness and gaze upon the sigil. Ask it to support you in achieving this intention. Now each time you use this sigil, state the intention to yourself. The more you use it, the more powerful it will become!

Moon water

Moon water is another tool that often gets unnecessarily complicated in spiritual spaces. It is simply water infused with the moon's energy. That's it. We don't have to make it a physics exam. You can make moon water during ANY phase of the moon; just be sure it's a phase you WANT to work with. Here are some questions to ask yourself before making moon water:

- **How are my energy levels affected by this moon phase?** Am I feeling energized, motivated, generally good overall? Or am I feeling drained, tired, emotional? If you feel like crap, you probably don't want to bottle up that energy and work with it throughout the month.

- **How do I want to use this moon water?** Remember, full moons are aligned with cleansing, so full moon water is great to add to your laundry or mop water to cleanse your space. New moon water is great for manifesting your intentions and goals, so you may want to use it when you meal prep your soups for the week or to water your plants.

Making moon water couldn't be easier—you just put water in any vessel (glass, plastic, ceramic—it does not matter!) and simply place it either outside or on a windowsill. Before you start overthinking it, here are answers to some common questions about moon water:

- No, it does not need to be in view of the moon. The moon's energy still impacts us when it's cloudy out, so don't stress about that.

- You can keep it out there as long as you want. I usually bring it in when I wake up, while some people opt to do a meditation outside under the moon for a few minutes and then bring it inside. Don't stress about the sun coming up; it won't ruin your moon water. After all, the light of the moon is a reflection of the sun.

- Be mindful of the vessel you use if you're in a freezing climate so it doesn't shatter. Keep it inside on your windowsill if temperatures are dropping.

- You can keep moon water however long you want; it does not expire.

- You can use it in A LOT of different ways—basically anywhere you use water. I'll share my favorite uses for moon water throughout this book.

Crystals

Whether you are a seasoned crystal collector or just think they're pretty, crystals can be an easy and powerful way to add intention and Magic to everyday tasks. From placing them alongside your skincare products to keeping them by your desk to remind you not to blow up on your coworkers, crystals are simple reminders of your intention. Below are just a few crystals used for common intentions; you will find a more comprehensive list in the Crystal Appendix (page 297) and the Ingredients by Intention (page 301) at the back of the book.

SELF-LOVE	ABUNDANCE	PROTECTION
Rose quartz	Pyrite	Jet
Rhodonite	Green aventurine	Onyx
Green aventurine	Jade	Black tourmaline
Pink or green stones	Yellow or gold stones	Black or gray stones
Clear quartz	Clear quartz	Clear quartz

CLEANSING	LUCK	CALM	CLARITY
Selenite	Jade	Sodalite	Fluorite
Amethyst	Pyrite	Celestite	Amethyst
Celestite	Citrine	Amethyst	Smoky quartz
Crystal clusters	Tiger's-eye	Blue stones	Sodalite
Clear quartz	Clear quartz	Clear quartz	Clear quartz

If you find yourself stranded on a deserted island, I recommend bringing clear quartz with you. Clear quartz is known as the master healer and can be used for most intentions. It amplifies whatever intention you give it, yet another reason why your intention is the most important ingredient to make something Magic. If you're new to crystals, start by collecting one from each of the above intentions, or simply begin with a single clear quartz.

Herbs and other Magical correspondences

Throughout the book I'll be offering you ways to add Magic to your chores based on the ingredients you're already using. For instance, if you have a mint-scented shampoo, you can turn that into a spell for mental clarity. This also comes up quite a bit in the kitchen section of the book. Below is a sample of different Magical correspondences based on intentions; you'll find a more comprehensive Ingredients by Intention in the appendix at the back of the book (page 301).

SELF-LOVE	ABUNDANCE	PROTECTION
Rose	Cinnamon	Salt
Chamomile	Mint	Pepper
Strawberry	Basil	Garlic
Rhubarb	Oregano	Sage
Rosemary	Rosemary	Rosemary

CLEANSING	LUCK	CALM	CLARITY
Lemon	Cinnamon	Mint	Mint
Orange	Clove	Lavender	Fennel
Salt	Basil	Chamomile	Lemon
Parsley	Chamomile	Lemon balm	Carrot
Rosemary	Rosemary	Rosemary	Rosemary

Notice something in common? Yep, rosemary can be used as an herb for most intentions. Think of it like the Uno wild card of

Magical ingredients. You'll also notice that some herbs can be used for multiple purposes. It's your intention that determines whether your cinnamon, for instance, is being used for abundance or luck (or BOTH). How do you decide? Go with what makes sense for you—if you're allergic to cinnamon, use something else with a similar intention! Also use what you have on hand; no need to buy a bunch of stuff to make this work. Let your intuition guide you—remember, *you are the Magic!*

Reiki and energy healing

Our final ingredient requires using your hands to imbue objects (or yourself) with universal energy. The practice I'm trained in is called Reiki, which is a Japanese energy-healing practice that reduces stress, helps with healing, and increases relaxation. Reiki has been proven effective at regulating the nervous system, aka switching out of that fight/flight/freeze response and into the relaxation response, so I'm a big advocate for it. But if you're not familiar with Reiki, don't stress! You can use your own energy to infuse intentions instead.

Below is a simplified tutorial for directing energy through your hands:

1. Hold your hand on or above whatever you wish to infuse with positive, loving energy.

2. Take a deep breath and feel the support beneath your feet.

3. Notice how your body feels and allow yourself to come into the present moment.

4. Now call in your intention. Feel it within your body and heart.

5. As you breathe in, allow that intention to expand throughout your body.

6. As you exhale, feel that intention drip down your arms and out through your hands.

7. Repeat for as many breaths as you wish.

Now for the fun part:

These tools set the foundation for our Mundane Magic practice, but they are only the beginning. Go ahead and flip now to the room you want to start in and dive into the Daily Rituals for that space.

STOP HERE!

Before moving on to the exercises in this book, you should first check in with your needs.

Tuning in to what you need physically, emotionally, mentally, and energetically at any given moment is the most important self-care task. While this isn't always easy to do, each time you stop and check in, you give yourself the gift of your awareness. Just as a bicycle needs regular maintenance, so do YOU! Have you ever ridden a bike and noticed the chain getting a little stuck but most of the time it's fine? This is a sign that maintenance will be needed soon. We know instinctively that if we ignore this sign, one day the chain may totally break and our bicycle will be out of commission until it gets fixed.

Our body offers similar clues to what maintenance is needed, but often we ignore them. We go through life on autopilot and end up only stopping when we get sick or injured. Regularly checking in on your needs not only helps you prevent a premature breakdown, but also strengthens your intuition! Try the following meditation each morning for a week and see how you feel.

MEDITATION

Tune In and Tune Up

Start by finding a comfortable seat or lying down. Take a few deep breaths to settle in, and notice the support underneath your body.

Feel the support beneath your feet and legs. Feel the textures beneath your fingertips and the temperature of the room on your skin.

Now scan your body from head to toe, noticing any sensations that are here. These may be subtle sensations like the feeling of clothing against your skin or a light pulsing beneath the surface of your body. Or they may be more obvious sensations: tugging, tension, aching, or even pain. The goal here isn't to change anything you're feeling; simply notice with curiosity what's here.

Now bring your attention to those achy, tense sensations that might be in the body. What would it be like to breathe into this part of the body? Imagine your inhale could stretch this part of the body out, taking up space beneath the skin. And with each exhale, relax this part of your body as much as you're able.

Bring your awareness now to the state of your mind. Perhaps your brain feels busy or scattered; maybe you feel spacious and at peace; you could also be somewhere in between. Noticing with curiosity what's going on up there between your ears?

Is there a worry or thought that's looping on autopilot through your brain? If so, take a breath and inhale space into your thoughts. With each exhale, imagine you could release that thought out of your mind into the space around you.

Now tune in to your heart space. Is there an emotion, or several, present in your body right now? Where do you feel it in your physical body? How does that emotion show up in your mind?

Place your hands over your heart space and offer the gift of your curious attention to this emotion. Allow it to show up fully, to take up space in your body, to be acknowledged.

Take a deep breath into your heart space and exhale out your mouth. Offer a moment of gratitude for yourself for taking this time to tune in to your needs and tune up your body, mind, and heart before tackling your to-do list.

Now open your eyes and begin your day.

Chapter 3

Living Room

Welcome to the living room—a space where you likely spend quite a bit of time. Whether you're watching TV, reading a book, entertaining guests, or playing a board game, the living room is one of the most utilized spaces in your home. Look around your living room. What do you notice? This space energetically reflects our sense of connection, communication, and joy.

When your living room is cluttered, you might notice difficulty connecting to others, especially those in your household, or your home may feel more chaotic overall. On the other hand, a living room that is too pristine and sterile can make your home feel like you're living in a hotel, creating a disconnect between you and your space. So it is important to keep the energy in this space in balance for the overall health of you and your home.

Energy accumulates in a space much like dust, pollen, or pet hair. As annoying as those dust bunnies are, they can be a great indicator of how clear the energy in your space actually is. When you start to notice dust building up, it's time to clear the energy of the space. And, spoiler alert, as you physically clean your space, you energetically clean it as well.

As we move into the living room, focus on how the energy of the space feels in your body before and after each task. You'll likely notice that, as the energy and debris clear, you feel lighter and more motivated to move on to the rest of the house!

Daily Rituals

Exercise

Exercise gets a bad rap, probably because we are so inundated with diet culture that the words *exercise* and *shame* go hand in hand—especially if you live in a bigger body or don't fit societal standards of beauty. But the truth is, exercise is a powerful energy-clearing practice that has nothing to do with dieting or counting calories. Instead of moving your body to "exercise," what if you moved your body to shake out stagnant energy? What if you found a type of movement you actually ENJOY, instead of forcing yourself to exercise because you "should"?

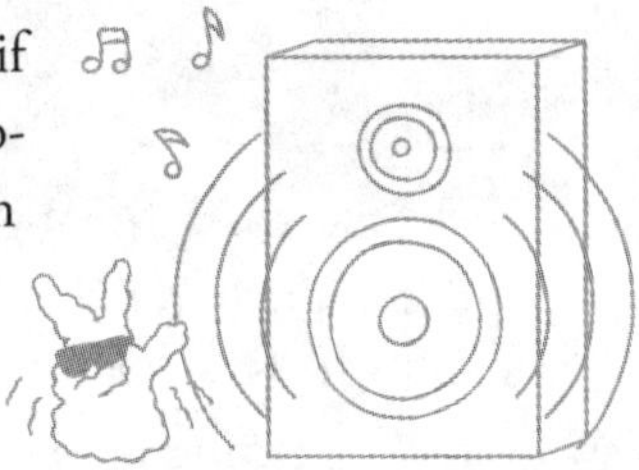

Movement doesn't have to be at a gym. It could be dancing in your living room, taking a walk to get yourself a Little Treat Magic, or cleaning your house. Heck, if you start to implement the rituals in this book, you're likely getting more movement than usual! Take the pressure off yourself and start moving to clear your energy.

Now, if you need a bit of motivation to get started, Color Magic can be a huge help. Red or orange are great colors for motivation and activating that inner fire to get moving. You could choose a coordinating outfit or add a red sticker to your water bottle. As always, make this as big or small as you need!

Don't forget to hydrate while you move. Filling your water bottle with moon water can add a little extra pizzazz to your workout. If you don't have moon water, don't worry—you can set your water bottle on your windowsill at night and *BOOM* now you do!

Finally, a few crystals can help light a fire under your feet to get moving: carnelian is great for motivation and energy, and a personal favorite of mine to take to the gym. Ancient warriors brought carnelian into battle to support their courage, so if you have any nerves about starting a new workout routine, hold carnelian to help you!

Stretching

Did you know that energy moves within your body through a connective tissue called your *myofascial system,* or *fascia*? This is a tangible web of tissue that connects your whole body from head to toe, and it's responsible for sending information from body to mind and back again. Because you're totally connected by this system, you might notice your back starting to hurt if you walk around wearing crappy shoes. This is due to tension moving up the chain as the fascia gets tugged and pulled in different directions.

An energetic block occurring in, say, your throat (maybe because you haven't been asking for what you need or communicating your true feelings) can also create tension elsewhere in your body. That energetic block creates a tug on the fascia, which can be felt all over.

When you stretch, see if you can trace the way energy becomes squeezed and released. What parts of your body feel tight and how does the tightness impact your mind and energy as you stretch this area? Becoming aware of WHERE you hold physical tension can give you a clue to what emotional needs are not being met. As you stretch, imagine releasing that tension and notice how that impacts you emotionally. Here's a chart to help you get started:

WHERE YOU HOLD TENSION	POSSIBLE EMOTIONAL CAUSES
Feet, legs, lower back	Excessive worry, basic needs not being met (food, shelter, financial security), family issues
Hips, pelvis	Creative blocks, lack of passion, losing the zest of life, betrayal of trust
Stomach, mid back, ribs	Low self-esteem, self-doubt, lack of motivation or confidence
Chest, shoulders, upper back	Grief, lack of connection to others, carrying emotional burdens of others, burnout
Neck, throat, jaw	Not speaking your truth, lack of boundaries, lying (to self or others)
Eyes, head, brain	Anxiety, addictive thinking, inability to perceive all sides of a situation, tunnel vision on a problem or worry, lack of connection to spirituality, loneliness

Magical Upkeep

Clearing clutter

There's nothing stagnant energy loves more than CLUTTER—and as an ADHD girlie with an affinity for collecting far too many rocks and books, I know how hard it can be to keep the clutter at bay. So here are a few ways to make your decluttering more Magical, no matter where the clutter is lingering. If you don't know where to begin, start with the Five-Minute Clutter-Crushing Charm below.

Five-Minute Clutter-Crushing Charm

This is the perfect starting place. The goal here is not to make your space perfect; it's to build momentum.

Your goal is to set a timer for five minutes and practice tuning in to the energy of your space and the energy within yourself. In these five minutes, you'll explore how changes in your environment affect that energy while intentionally tidying up your space. Use the following meditation anytime you need a blast of motivation OR as a wind-down ritual for your space before bed.

MEDITATION

Clutter-Crushing Charm*

*For a guided audio version of this meditation, visit mollydonlan.com/resources.

To begin, put your feet on the floor. That's it. That's step number one.

As you put your feet on the floor, begin to take an inventory of how your energy feels in the space that you're in.

Is there a density to the energy in certain parts of your space? Is there a lightness in some areas?

Let's start in the part of the space that feels most dense and just walk your way over to that space. No rush. We don't need to completely solve all the problems in your space right now.

Pick up one item in that part of your space that doesn't belong there. Maybe it belongs in a different room. Maybe it belongs in the trash can or the laundry. Maybe there's another part of the room that it belongs in.

If it belongs somewhere else in the room, go ahead and put it away. If it belongs somewhere else entirely, go ahead and place it on the threshold of your room—the doorway or hallway. But don't leave the room.

Try this for a few minutes in the part of your space that feels most dense.

Notice if you're feeling a shift in the energy of that one little pocket of your space.

Maybe you feel the density shift to the threshold of your room. That's okay for now. Don't worry about that.

Take an inventory of the room once again, and just notice where you feel density. Start moving and clearing that part of the space, following the energy.

Where does it feel dense? Pick up things and put them away if they're in the room, and just place them on the threshold if they belong outside the room.

That's it. Don't leave the room, lest you get distracted by the energy of other spaces. Simply move through your room, picking up things, putting them where they belong, or placing them on the threshold.

And as you do this, notice: Do you feel a shift of energy within you? Know that your energy and the energy of your environment go hand in hand.

Maybe if you're feeling that density around you, you're feeling it within. So now take a deep breath and clear the clutter out from within.

You're over halfway through. So tune in, notice: How is your space feeling?

Be realistic with yourself. *What's one more area of the space I can tackle in the next two minutes?* Don't rush.

Remember: two minutes a day is more effective than sixty minutes once a month when it comes to cleaning our home and cleaning our energy. In fact, any spiritual practice that you do is more effective in these small doses than in the big hauls every once in a while.

Give yourself credit for even showing up this far.

Now come back to the center of your space. Can you tune in to the energy? Has anything changed? Maybe there's a little bit of lightness where there once was density. Maybe it feels like the energy has moved or is moving.

Now let yourself tune in to anything that's shifted within you and your body, your mind, your momentum, your motivation.

The hardest part is starting, and you already did that. As you complete this practice, bring yourself to anything that's on the threshold. If it's garbage, you're going to throw it away. Otherwise, all you're going to do is bring it to the room that it belongs in. You don't have to put it away. Just bring it to its home.

If they're dishes, bring them to the kitchen.
If it's laundry, bring it to the laundry basket.
If it's something else, bring it to wherever it belongs.

You did it. Congratulations. Take a deep breath in and let a full breath out.

Shoe and stuff mountain by the front door

Consider your front door the energetic entry into your home. By keeping mountains of "stuff" here, you're blocking the path for fresh, abundant energy to enter your home. Instead, create a mini altar here—place a houseplant on a small table to protect and cleanse the energy of your home, and surround it with a few crystals like black tourmaline or selenite to keep the energy from stagnating. When you have a beautiful and intentional altar in place, you'll be less likely to throw a bunch of junk on top of it. Now you can place your shoes neatly under the altar table so that the altar's energy cleanses the outside energy off your shoes, preventing it from spreading throughout your house.

Organize bags/purses/coats

If you have a closet in your living room, you may be tempted to pack so much stuff in there that it busts out cartoon-style whenever you open the door. In this closet you likely keep coats, bags, purses, and other outerwear. This is an excellent opportunity to create a bit of Protection Magic. Outerwear is our first layer of energetic defense against the elements and other people's energy; keeping it hung up neatly helps prevent that energy from getting trapped. Use the idea of protection as motivation to get some hangers and organize your jackets! Finally, purses and bags are a representation of your abundance. Keeping them neat, cleaned out, and organized encourages more abundance to come your way. Before you shove a bag into your closet of doom, give it a good clean-out. Throw out the old receipts and trash, then give your bag a quick smoke cleanse before tucking it away neatly. Smoke cleansing is a practice of using the smoke of an incense stick, herb bundle, or other fire to clear the energy of an object or space. Simply waft the smoke in and around the bag; you don't have to worry about getting the smoke into every nook and cranny, but do be sure not to light it on fire. Bonus—if you can stand the scent of cinnamon, these sticks are awesome to use for smoke cleansing your purses as a way to invite even more abundance into your life!

Catchall table or coffee table

Other than the couch (discussed starting on page 78), the coffee table is the center of your living space and so it often turns into a catchall table likely filled with dishes, books, paperwork, stray earrings, and pet hair. When you clear off the energy in the center of your space, it allows the energy in your entire space to move. Think of it like turning on a ceiling fan, moving the energy from the inside out. To make clearing off this part of your space more Magical, add some moon water to your all-purpose cleaners—or better yet, stick the all-purpose cleaner on your windowsill overnight to make the entire thing into moon water! Now add a crystal or a tarot deck to the center of your coffee table to help keep the energy clear. Bonus—this will remind you to preserve this space for good energetic flow rather than allowing things to pile up again!

Organize bookshelves

Think of your bookshelves like mini altars. An altar is a dedicated space designed with reverence that serves as a focal point for a specific intention. Altars can imbue your space with positive energy or they can weigh your space down. Do a little purge of your bookshelves and ask yourself, *Does this book still serve me in some way?* Separate the books into *Yes, No,* and *Maybe* piles. Wipe down the empty shelves with moon water and begin arranging the books from the *Yes* pile in a way that makes your intuition smile and makes the energy in this part of the room feel spacious rather than stagnant. Finally, set the *Maybe* books aside for now. If you have space on your shelf, you can add them in. Or you can repeat the process to discern which ones you really feel like keeping. Any that still feel like *Maybe*s can be tucked away for a few weeks to soften any emotional attachments you may have to them; then you can reassess with a clear head! Take books from the *No* pile to a Little Free Library for someone else to enjoy—as a bonus, this gets you to take a short walk and become more familiar with your community.

Returning library books

Library books are such a beautiful expression of gratitude and Little Treat Magic! Utilizing your local public library or Little Free Library is a gratitude practice for this amazing and essential service that's provided to your community.

When you pick up a library book, give it a gentle cleanse using sound by ringing a bell over it or playing some music to it. As you enjoy the book, consider the emotions it brings to you and the places the story transports you to. Hold these things energetically as you close the book for the final time.

By returning your library books, you offer the next person in line the opportunity to receive a little treat of reading it sooner. Add a bookmark with a loving note to the book before returning it, a treasure for the next reader or the librarian to find. As you drop the book off, wish it well on its next adventure, infusing it with your positive energy or even sending the book a bit of Reiki before releasing it to the library again. Think of this like creating an energetic book club, connecting the book next with its perfect reader!

After you return your book, energetically release all attachments to the book, trusting that it will go to the perfect person next! Now give yourself a Little Treat Magic by picking up a new book to read, or make a day out of it and hunker down at your favorite coffee shop with a cozy drink to read for the afternoon uninterrupted.

Cleaning up after pets

Pets can be messy. From dog hair on the couch to bird poop on the carpet, we can see the mess as a source of frustration or as a source of inspiration. Did you know you can save feathers, whiskers, or even pet hair that has naturally been shed and use them for spells? Using these items in a protection spell or health spell can impact you AND your pet in positive ways.

Consider making a protection spell jar for your pet! Grab some pet hair, a fallen whisker, a claw clipping, or a discarded feather from your friend and place it in a jar with protective herbs, crystals, and salt. Keep it in your home near your pet's food or medication.

When you're out and notice pet hair all over your pants, instead of jumping to try to wipe it off immediately, take a moment to reflect on gratitude for your pet's love. See their love envelop your entire body, protecting you from negative energies when you're out and about.

Decluttering pet toys

This is a great game to strengthen your intuition and interact with your pet! Gather all of your pet's toys into a bin and sit with your pet. Grab two toys at a time and use your intuition to guess which toy they will choose. Lay them in front of your pet with space between and notice which toy they gravitate toward first. Continue until you've shown your pet each toy, and donate or toss the toys that don't get chosen.

Donating clutter

Have you ever heard of the "poop rule" when decluttering? The poop rule is a way to help release attachment to items you wouldn't normally keep around. Essentially, when going through items, you hold an item and ask yourself, *If this had poop on it, would I clean it off and keep it?* If the answer is no, donate it. As a witch, I prefer the candle wax rule . . . If you've ever spilled a seven-day candle on your desk, you know what a pain it is to get the wax off literally everything. As you pick through your items, would you go through the pain of cleaning candle wax off it? If not, donate it!

As you bring your items to donate, feel gratitude for them and how they have served you. Let them go with gratitude so they can bless someone else!

The couch

Your couch is likely the central part of your living room. It's also probably where you spend the most time when you are in that room; therefore, it holds the most energy in that room. Have you ever noticed times when you felt glued to the couch, dissociated and scrolling on your phone until the wee hours of the morning? Despite wanting to get up and do something else, you can't seem to pry yourself away. I like to call this energetic "glue" that goops up on the couch and keeps you stuck and stagnant. One of the best ways to remove this "glue" is to do a deep energetic clean of the couch.

Start by moving the couch so you can access beneath it. Simply moving a piece of furniture will revitalize the energy of the room. Now you can physically see the energy that's stuck underneath where you sit, and you can vacuum or sweep to clean this energy out.

Now remove the cushions and wash the blankets, again noticing the tangible evidence of stagnant energy in your couch in the form of crumbs, dust, and other debris. You've been marinating in it each time you sit down. Vacuum this up—you may already feel a difference now!

Finally, refold the blankets, rearrange the pillows, spritz a bit of moon water over the couch cushions, and bask in the fresh energy you've created! You may even notice the room looks brighter! Simply doing this last step each day can keep that energetic "glue" from settling and give you a burst of momentum to do something other than sit on the couch.

But remember: sometimes vegging out is exactly what we need, so there's no shame in that. Just be sure that you're making a conscious choice and not getting stuck because of stagnant energy in your couch holding you back!

Caring for houseplants

If you're anything like me, the state of your plants is a reflection of the state of your mental health. Plants also impact the energy of your space and your emotional state. When they're doing well, you feel better. By making your plant-watering routine more Magical, you can help keep your plant friends thriving!

Start by making watering them a routine—I like to align this with the new and full moons, but you may need to do more or less depending on your plants' needs. Using the lunar cycle to water your plants is also great because you can water them with your moon water!

Consider your plants as energetic air purifiers. Just as their leaves transform carbon dioxide into oxygen to purify the air of your space, plants also purify and protect the energy of your home. Let their leaves be an indicator of when you need to refresh them so they can continue keeping your home's energy safe! When the leaves get dusty, give them a gentle wash with moon water. And when they need a pruning, offer them gratitude for protecting your space and taking on unhelpful energy so you don't have to.

When repotting plants, consider using Color Magic to choose the plant pot. A plant potted in black is great for the front door to protect the energy of your home; green plant pots in the kitchen can invite in more abundance; and blue plant pots in the bedroom can help you sleep!

Finally, add some crystals to your plant pots to keep your plants healthy! Rose quartz is great for plants that tend to lose leaves or wilt often; clear quartz can help plants grow; moss agate can help maintain your plants' health; and citrine in a plant pot can help your manifestations grow as the plant does.

Cleaning the TV screen

Craving clarity in your life? Use your TV screen to help you find it. As with the cable organization task (see page 88), when we focus on clearing the TV screen we can see this mirrored in our mental processes, too.

Steep yourself a cup of peppermint tea while you use a soft, dry cloth to wipe the dust and smudges from your TV screen and frame. Imagine with each swipe that your mind becomes clearer and clearer.

Trust that, even if the answer doesn't appear to you immediately, this process will carve a path for it to arrive when it's meant to. Finally, seal up this practice by stirring a sigil for mental clarity into your tea, then pop your fave TV show on while you drink it!

Vacuuming

No matter what, vacuuming SUCKS! Let's make it a little easier with a few very simple shifts.

Remember that your vacuum is literally an energy-clearing device: it sucks up stagnant energy and refreshes the space instantly. You can amplify this by adding a few drops of essential oils to a cotton ball and vacuuming it up. Not only will this make your space smell great, but the scent will be a tangible indicator that the energy in that part of your home has been cleared. Bonus—you can choose your scent based on the Magical correspondences (see Ingredients by Intention, page 301) and spread a specific intention throughout your space.

On the topic of spreading an intention throughout the space, drawing sigils on your vacuum is a great way to add Magic to an otherwise boring task. You can use a marker or sticky note on your stand-up vac, or if you have a robot vacuum you can draw a sigil on it with masking tape. Now every time your vacuum moves through the room, the intention of your sigil will spread through the space as well!

Finally, let's reframe vacuuming with a bit of Magical mindset. This is one of those chores that are great to do before the start of the week so you walk into your Monday to-do list with fresh energy OR on the full moon to clear out stagnant energy and align with the lunar cycle. No matter when you vacuum, the amount of energy you'll be moving out of your space is guaranteed to help you bust out of a rut and find motivation again.

Sweeping

It's no secret that witches love brooms, but did you know you can change the energy of your space by sweeping in specific ways?

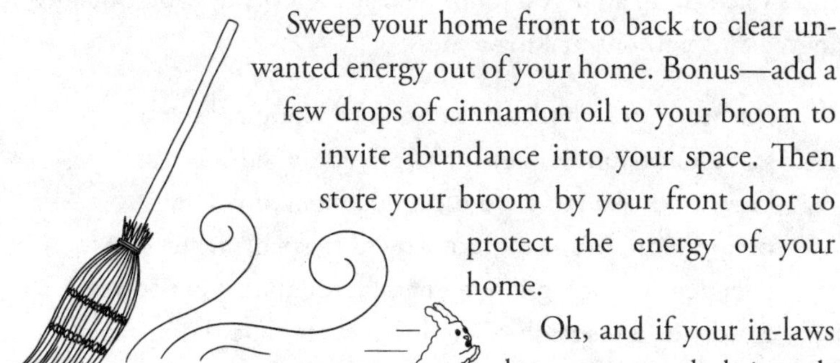

Sweep your home front to back to clear unwanted energy out of your home. Bonus—add a few drops of cinnamon oil to your broom to invite abundance into your space. Then store your broom by your front door to protect the energy of your home.

Oh, and if your in-laws have overstayed their welcome, flip your broom upside down so the bristles face up to banish their energy from the space.

Finally, when you move, leave your old broom behind and get a new one. That way, you're not carrying the energy of your old space into the new.

Mopping

Ugh, everyone hates to mop. BUT if you're into Magic, chances are the joy of making potions will resonate with you. Now, whether you've made a potion in your life lately, I'm willing to bet you were a kid who enjoyed mixing together random concoctions from supplies you found under the bathroom cabinet. We're going to use this spark of childhood experimentation to make mopping more Magical!

Instead of filling your mop bucket with soap and water (boring), fill it with a soap and water POTION (fun)! This is a great opportunity to set an intention for your home and spread it throughout your space as you mop. If you want to get extra fancy, practice drawing sigils on the floor with your mop as you clean.

For your mopping potion, you can use any number of ingredients, but be sure you add them in with both intention and function in mind. For instance, you don't want to throw a cup of lavender flowers in with your soap and then make an even bigger mess to clean up after you mop. Here are a few ways you can add ingredients without making a mess:

- **Herbs:** Choose herbs based on their Magical correspondences and either simmer them on the stove or brew them like tea before adding them to your mopping potion. This is a great way to reuse a simmer pot to continue spreading the intention throughout your space. Simply add a splash of the herby water into the bucket with your soap and water.

- **Crystals:** Make sure you choose water-safe crystals OR create an indirect water infusion as described in Chapter 5 (see page 124).

- **Soap bases:** You can use whatever mopping soap you have on hand OR grab one based on the Magical properties. For instance, pine-scented floor cleaner is great for purification and intuition; mint soaps are great for clarity of mind and energy; lavender soaps are great for peace and relaxation; cherry blossom scents could be used for new beginnings.

- **Essential oils:** You can add spell oils or essential oils to your mopping potion, but be sure you use them in small amounts—we don't want to create a Slip 'N Slide situation! Note that if you have pets in the home, please be sure whatever you add to your mopping potion is pet-safe and properly diluted.

Following are a few recipes to get you started; you'll find even more in the appendix of this book (page 287).

As with any of the recipes in this book, the goal is to use what you have. Don't have lavender soap but have lavender essential oil? Cool, substitute it. Don't feel like you need to buy a bunch of stuff to make these! Unscented soap can be substituted for any of the scented options; just add the scent noted into your herbal infusion instead.

You'll also note there are no suggested amounts for the ingredients. This is intentional. For the soaps, follow the directions on the bottle based on the size of your bucket. For the herbs and oils, a few drops are fine, but you can use more or less based on your preferences. Let yourself PLAY and have FUN with this, rather than thinking you need a lot of structure to make it work.

Calm and Peaceful Home Mopping Potion

- **Lavender-scented soap** *to calm the mind*
- **Chamomile flowers** *to invite in peace*
- **Amethyst** *to promote rest*

Clear Thinking and Focus Mopping Potion

- **Lemon-scented soap** *to clear the clutter of your mind*
- **Peppermint essential oil** *to invite clarity*
- **Fluorite for focus** *(Use the indirect infusion method described on page 124)*

Self-Love Mopping Potion

- **Rose-scented soap** *to connect with your heart*
- **Hibiscus tea** *to draw in self-love to your heart*
- **Rose quartz** *to amplify your connection to self*

New Home Blessing and Protection Mopping Potion

- **Pine-scented soap** *to clear away anyone else's energy*
- **Cinnamon** *for luck and prosperity*
- **Basil** *for protection*
- **Clear quartz** *to amplify the spell*

Dusting

Dust is an indicator that energy has had an opportunity to settle in your space. The things in your living room that move often (like the remote control) almost never accumulate dust, but the TV stand does because the energy stagnates there. By dusting, you are clearing out stagnant energy—the kind of energy that leaves us feeling unmotivated, fatigued, and overall blah. At the same time, you can use dusting as an opportunity to replace that stagnant energy with a specific intention.

For example, you can use a bit of moon water on a damp rag or in your spray cleaner when you dust to cleanse the energy of your space and add in the intention you set with the lunar cycle. You could also add an herbal infusion or a few drops of leftover simmer pot water to your spray cleaner to add an additional layer of intention to your dusting routine.

Finally, you may want to draw a sigil into the dust before sweeping it away. Think of it as setting an intention in each of the spaces in your living room as you clean.

Deep Magic

Cleaning baseboards

This task pairs great with the full moon! Though they may not need to be cleaned every week, your baseboards will start to accumulate dust over time. And remember: where there is dust, there is stagnant energy keeping you from accessing your motivation and potential!

Grab your fave mopping potion (see pages 84 and 287) and a rag. After cleaning the floors of the space, wash the baseboards using the same mopping potion and a rag. Feel the stagnant energy completely dissolve from every nook and cranny of your space, with your intention filling the space instead. Cleanse the energy of your baseboards and feel yourself align with the full moon at the same time! This is especially great if you struggle to stay grounded and present during the full moon: the baseboards are the energetic foundation of your walls, so keeping that energy clean can help you feel more grounded and settled internally, too.

Washing walls

If you're in an energetic rut of sorts—meaning you feel unmotivated, stuck, or just kind of blahhhh—this is one Magical task that is sure to bust you out of it! Now, washing your walls may not be something you do regularly—heck, maybe you've never done it EVER, in which case there's so much energy settled on them and impacting the energy in your space without even realizing it! By clearing this energy and setting a new intention in its place, you'll feel a visceral shift in your own energy each time you enter the space.

Grab your mop and make a mopping potion like you did for the floors. Now, with a clean mop head, dunk it into your mop bucket and wring it out REALLY good. Begin scrubbing the walls from top to bottom in your space. If you want to get really fancy, you can take down pictures or anything else on the walls. If you need to quickly spruce up the energy in your space, simply adjust the picture frames so they're not tilted. When your space comes into alignment, your energy comes into alignment, so aligning the picture frames is a great way to make this happen without much effort!

Finally, once the walls are clean, take a step back and notice the energy in the room. Has anything shifted? How do you know? Where do you feel it in your body?

Shampooing carpets and upholstery

The soft, squishy areas of your home hold more energy than more dense, slick surfaces. So shampooing your carpets, rugs, and furniture counts as more of an energetic deep clean. This is a great solstice/equinox ritual to help transition energetically into the next season. Or, if you need to do it more often, you can opt to make it a full moon ritual.

Choose the scent of your shampoo or soap by the Magical correspondences (see Ingredients by Intention, page 301) for the intention you want to bring into your space. You could also add a few drops of essential oils or herbal infusions to the soap mix—just make sure to spot-test first so you don't accidentally cause stains! Here are a few examples of scents:

- **Lavender:** Invites peace, relaxation, calm
- **Citrus:** Invites energy, joy; cleanses the energy
- **Mint:** Encourages clarity, abundance, and clear communication

Cleaning windows

Windows are portals—think of how the sunlight streams into your space through the glass. Now imagine you were to draw a sigil on the glass—that sunlight would infuse with the sigil's energy and spread the intention throughout your space! When you're washing your windows, draw a sigil on the glass with your rag before wiping it away.

To add even more Magic, use moon water with your glass cleaner! Finally, if you want that sigil to last even longer, consider drawing it in clear nail polish on the window frame. It's subtle enough that only you will know it's there, but the energy will be felt by all!

Make sure that when you clean the windows, you don't neglect the energetic buildup on the blinds and curtains. Toss curtains in the wash with some moon water, wipe down blinds with the same, or simply spritz some moon water on them if you're in a pinch!

Organizing cables

How we do anything is how we do everything means our physical bodies can be reflected in our physical space and vice versa. This is a fantastic ritual for when you're feeling tension in the body. Think of the tangled-up tissues of your body where energy isn't able to flow, causing the tension to build up. You can begin to untangle inside by untangling outside your body.

As you untangle the cables and cords in your living room, imagine your physical body untangling the tension it's been holding. As you reorganize the cables, feel the energy flowing more smoothly through your physical body. Let the cables be a representation of how you're feeling physically and notice if you feel a shift after realigning them!

Seasonal decorations

Do you ever feel kinda blah right around the season shifts? Often it's because the energy around us is changing but our environment still feels stagnant. This is a great opportunity to change out that seasonal decor and thus invite new energy that's aligned with the season coming up! Before you ask, YES, this still applies even if you live in an area that doesn't have drastic seasonal changes in nature.

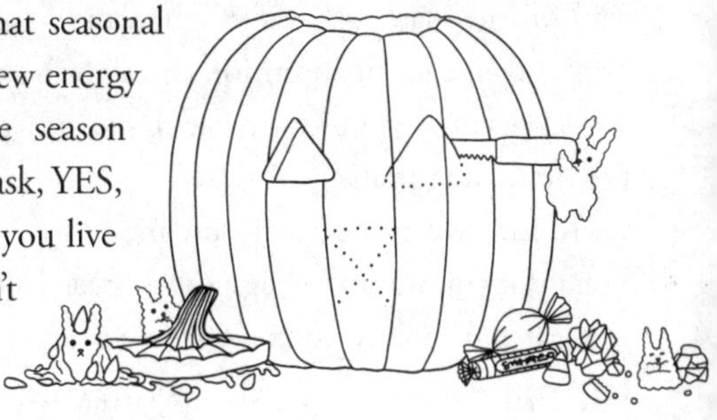

Here are a few ideas:

- **Spring:** The energy is about new beginnings and fresh momentum. As you decorate or undecorate your space, think about clearing away the dull energy of winter and inviting newness into your life through the decor in your space. Maybe add some fresh flowers to your altar or redecorate your space with greenery and plants. Let the colors of your decor be light and bright.

- **Summer:** This season is fiery and fast-moving with an outward focus. How can you make your space more inviting to visitors and turn the ideas you've been cooking up into a reality? Maybe you paint a room a new fun color, or maybe you just rearrange the pictures on your wall. Change up the colors to feel bolder and brighter. Let the decor create a feeling of new and bold energy!

- **Fall:** We begin turning inward and slowing down. How can you create more ease and let go of the go-go-go energy of summer? Add more cozy blankets to your space and let the colors in your home become more grounded and cool-toned.

- **Winter:** This is the most inward season of all, when the energy asks us to slow down and find stillness while reflecting on ourselves. Create an environment that invites reflection—candles or atmospheric touches bring comfort and ease; replace the overhead lights with twinkle lights; or add more sentimental touches to your space.

Cleaning ceiling fans and air vents

Whatever you use to circulate air in your space is a great way to circulate intention through your space as well. Clean your ceiling fan and air vents with multipurpose cleaner mixed with an essential oil or herb infusion that matches the intention you'd like to have in your space. To add even more intention to your space, draw sigils on the top side of your ceiling fan blades using your finger dipped in moon water, or use a marker to draw sigils on the air filters of your home.

Cleaning the fireplace

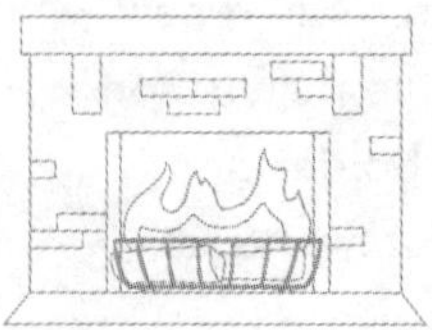

Your fireplace is just a giant example of Fire Magic. Fire can burn away unwanted energies, help you release what you're unnecessarily holding on to, and light the path for you to move forward. Keeping it tidy helps remove the residue of the energy it's constantly absorbing and moving for you.

This is a great full moon chore. As you empty out the soot and ash, think about everything you've been able to release over the last lunar cycle. You've already begun the process of letting it go by burning it; now finish the job by removing the ash from your space. Use some full moon water with soap to clean the glass or surrounding areas. Finally, once it's all clean, write down what you'd like to release over the next lunar cycle and burn it in the next fire!

Tending the animal cage

If you have a caged animal, their cage is an opportunity to create a mini ecosystem of energy for

them! Consider making a crystal grid around the cage to support your pet's health and happiness. If you have a paper liner in the cage, draw sigils on it! Is someone getting on your nerves? Write their name on the paper or print a photo of them to be pooped on. Want a fun divination practice to try with your pet? Write words on the paper at the bottom of their cage, then circle them. Notice where your animal does their business the most—what does that word mean to you, your home, or your pet?

Decorating the fish tank

Speaking of creating an ecosystem of energy—your fish's tank is the perfect place to do this! Choose rocks and other decorations using Color Magic. Assign energetic intentions to the decor based on its symbolism. Here are a few ideas to get you started, but feel free to make your own associations as well.

DECORATION	MAGICAL CORRESPONDENCES
Barnacles	Longevity, cleansing
Barrel	Resilience, transformation, maturity
Castle	Protection, abundance, growth
Pineapple	Courage, luck, confidence
Plants (real or fake)	Purification, replenishment, cleansing
Rocks	Grounding, support
Scuba diver	Wisdom, retention, relaxation
Ship	Adventure, teamwork
Treasure chest	Abundance, luck, prosperity
Volcano	Expansion, passion, energy

Chapter 4

Laundry Room

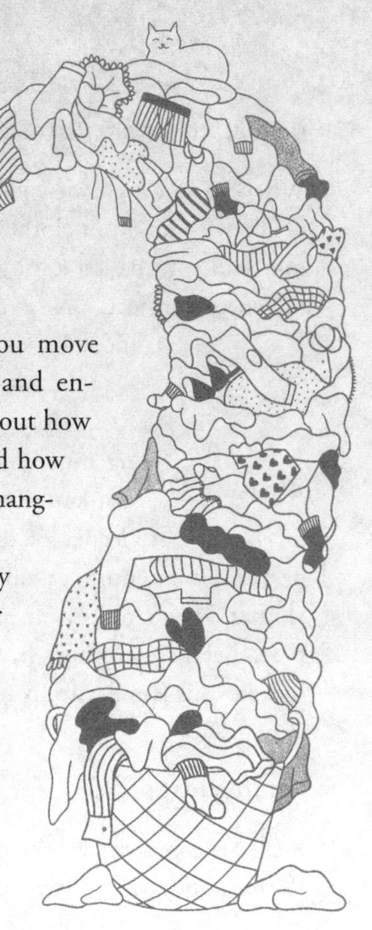

Your clothes are the barrier between you and the world, which means they pick up a TON of energy as you move through different environments and encounter different people. Think about how you feel after a long travel day and how much better you feel after simply changing your clothes.

All the chores in your laundry area are an opportunity to clear away any bad energy and to fortify the energetic protection that keeps your energy pure. Especially if you work in environments with a lot of stress and negativity, adding some Magic into your laundry routine can help you feel more emotionally resilient to the everyday stressors you encounter.

> "I love folding my family's clothes and coming up with affirmations as I touch each piece. For my kids' pajamas, I hug them and say, 'I am calm, I am safe, I am ready for rest.' And now my kids and I say that at bedtime, too. It has made the mundane task of laundry something to look forward to."
>
> —Sue T.

Daily Rituals

Collecting laundry around the house

When was the last time you cleansed your laundry hamper? Think of all the energy your clothes carry throughout the day—you drop that into your basket and then place clean clothes on top of that old energy. Instead, take a moment to cleanse the energy off your laundry basket and hamper. To do this, light an incense stick, give a spritz of moon water, or ring a bell. Cover the laundry basket with your cleansing medium of choice. Bonus point if you give your laundry basket a wipe-down with some kind of cleaner or disinfectant! Use your freshly cleaned basket as momentum to unload the dryer and put away your clean clothes. Now empty your hamper into the wash and cleanse this next. Before you know it, you have cleansed the energy AND moved your laundry to its final destination in your closet.

Finding lost socks

Really, this practice can be used to find anything, but while we're in the laundry room, we may as well find that lost sock! Grab a pendulum for this one—a pendulum is a weight hung from a fixed point that can swing back and forth. You may be picturing a crystal point on a chain, but did you know you can use anything as a pendulum?

Your phone charger can work in a pinch—hold the end you plug into your phone in your hand with a limp wrist, kind of like how you would hold a dead mouse by the tail. Let the charging block dangle.

Other household pendulums could include: necklaces with a bauble, hoodie string knotted at the end, keys on a lanyard, a belt with a buckle, a scarf or robe tie with one end knotted, a long sock with a rock in the toe.

Every pendulum is going to be a little different, so it's always good practice to begin by checking in with how the pendulum plans to communicate with you.

To begin, ask the pendulum, "Show me yes," and notice how it swings. It may be a back-and-forth motion or a circular motion. Notice which direction it moves: North to south? East to west? Clockwise? Counterclockwise?

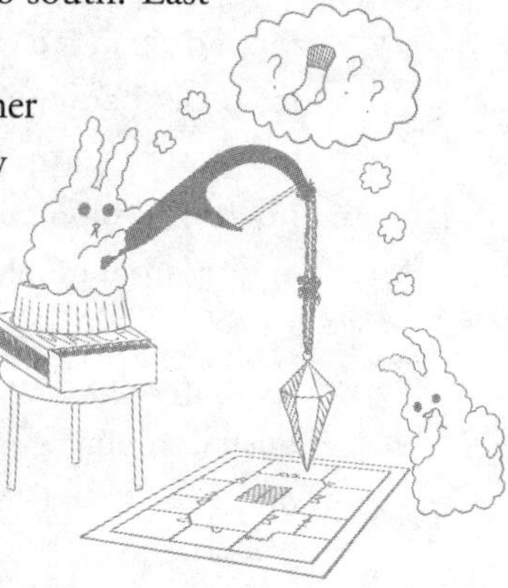

Now slow the pendulum with your other hand until it is centered again. Ask, "Show me no," and notice how it swings differently.

Now test the channel of communication by asking easy questions you already know the answer to. For instance, "Is my name [your name]?" should cause the pendulum to swing in the yes formation, and questions like "Do kangaroos speak Japanese fluently?" should swing in a no formation.

Once you've gotten to know your pendulum, it's ready to rock and roll. You can start using it to hunt for your missing object. Start with rooms in your house, asking yes-or-no questions. "Is it in the kitchen? Is it in the living room? Is it in the bedroom?" Move to the room that the pendulum directs you to.

You can ask follow-up questions once in the room—"Is it under something? Inside something? On top of something?"—or move around the room and ask, "Am I getting closer?"

Have fun as you explore this activity around your house!

Magical ways to use a single sock

Can't find that lost sock? Don't fret—you can use the single socks in your Mundane Magic practice! Here are a few ways to use a single sock:

- **Crystal storage:** Wrap your fragile crystals in a sock to protect them when moving or storing them.
- **DIY heating pad:** Fill a sock with dry rice and tie the top. Pop it in the microwave for thirty to sixty seconds for a DIY heating pad. Because rice cleanses and protects your energy, you can use it with the intention to purify any tension out of your body and protect your energy from others!
- **Dusting:** Slip a single sock over your hand to use in your dusting routine—make it Magical by following the steps on page 85 in Chapter 3!
- **Bath teas:** Fill a sock with herbs, Epsom salt, or oatmeal, then tie the top and toss it in your bath for a bath tea without the mess! You'll find a ton of recipes in the appendix (page 283).

- **Potpourri sachets:** Using the Ingredients Appendix (page 291) as your guide, fill a sock with herbs, spices, and dried fruits, and tie the top. Place it in your sock drawer or closet to infuse the space with scent and intention!
- **Insulation:** Slip a single sock around your iced coffee or iced tea cup to absorb condensation and insulate your spelled beverage!
- **Charm bags:** Fill a single sock with coins, baubles, herbs, crystals, and anything else that aligns with your intention, and tie it up. Keep it in your purse, car, or backpack for a portable spell jar alternative!
- **Deodorizing:** Fill a sock with baking soda and herbs, tie the top, and place it inside your shoes to cleanse the energy, remove odors, and infuse your shoes with intention.
- **Draft stopper:** For your longer socks, fill with dried rice and leftover dryer lint, and tie it off. Place at the gap of your doors to prevent drafts. Bonus if you add some protection herbs or crystals to protect your space at the same time!

Magical Upkeep

Stain removal

Banishing spells are intended to remove unwanted energy—whether that's releasing a song that's stuck in your head, an annoying telemarketer who won't stop calling, or the pervasive feeling of bleghhh you have after a long week. Banishment spells are traditionally done before larger spell work to purify the energy of the bigger ritual, just as stain removal must be done before the larger task of washing the laundry.

To begin, decide what energies you wish to banish. It could be as open as "any and all unwanted or unsupportive energies in my space" or something specific like "that annoying community solar solicitor who won't stop ringing my doorbell during important Zoom meetings."

Create an easy-to-remember statement for your banishment spell. Here are a few ideas to get you started:

- Any and all unwanted energies must leave my space now.
- I banish ________________________ and ask that the universe support me in blocking it/them from returning.
- With this spell, I erase ________________________ from my energy field.

You can create a sigil for this statement if you wish, or stick with the words alone. Now rub your stain remover in a counterclockwise direction while repeating the statement of banishment. When the stain is gone, your spell is complete.

Note: Some stains won't come out fully, but that doesn't mean your spell didn't work. Remember: YOU are the Magic and sometimes clothing stains for mundane reasons!

Washing your clothes

Perhaps the most important step to removing energy and grime from your clothing is washing them! Here are steps you can take to make washing your clothes more Magical while cleansing and protecting the energy of your clothing.

First, add a dash of moon water to your washer before starting a load of laundry to speed up the cleansing process. Next, add some Protection Magic to your washing soap. Draw a sigil for protection on the outside of the container, choose scents based on their Magical properties, or—if you're a DIY fan—make your own Magical washing potion with the recipe below.

Make your own laundry-washing potion

Wash away negative energy and add a layer of energetic protection by mixing the following ingredients into the wash along with your favorite detergent. As you do so, hold the intention that any unwanted energy be washed away and that your energy be protected from other energies when you next wear the garment.

- **Florida Water:** No, this isn't just tap water from Florida. This is a specific cologne that assists in cleansing energy. A few drops into the washer helps remove any negative energy!
- **Sun water:** Just as moon water is an infusion of the moon's energy, you can create an infusion of the sun's energy by leaving water out in sunlight. The sun is a powerful protector and therefore energetically great for this task! Place a cup of water on your windowsill while you collect laundry around your house, then toss it in with your detergent.
- **Essential oils:** Choose a scent that aligns with your intention and add a few drops to your wash. (Note: Take care when dropping these in so they don't stain your

garments! I usually prefer to drop them onto a rag and toss that in with my clothes.)

- **Vinegar:** Great for keeping clothes smelling clean and feeling softer—vinegar is also great for banishment! You only need about ⅛ to ¼ cup.

Cleaning the dryer vents

How's this for motivation: you can actually use dryer lint in your Magical practice—better start collecting!

Using lint in Magic spells

- Hold a ball of lint and direct any negative or unhelpful energy that you may have collected throughout the week into the ball. Now compost the lint and give the energy back to the earth in gratitude so it can be transmuted into new life.

- Create fire starters using old toilet paper rolls, leftover candles from spells, and lint. Use your fire starter to create a full moon firepit outside to release and let go of whatever no longer serves you.

- Stuff a proxy doll with lint, adding in crystals or baubles to represent the person you wish to send healing to. Once the doll is complete, offer a Reiki session to it with the intention that the energy flow at a distance to the person who wishes to receive it.

- Use lint as mulch to retain moisture in your witchy garden beds or line plant pots to retain moisture and plant a manifestation while you plant a physical seed. Watch both grow at the same time! (Be sure you don't use any toxic chemicals in your laundry if you choose this option!)

- Turn the lint into pulp and make your own paper for a Book of Shadows or manifestation paper. For manifestation paper, write what you desire, then burn or bury it to release it into the universe!

- Spin the lint into thread and knit it into a scarf while repeating an intention. Feel the intention absorbed into every stitch as you complete the craft. Now when you wear it, you're marinating in that energy!

- Use the lint as cushioning for storing crystals and other delicate Magical tools when not in use.

- Clean up spills on your altar—lint is especially great for absorbing your Magical oils and spilled candle wax!

- Make a spell jar using lint as a representation of your energy for a manifestation spell. Or use it as a way of making "static" between you and other people's energy for a protection spell jar.

Drying laundry

Remember to switch your laundry over

One of the more underrated energy-cleansing techniques is music. Often we think of only "spiritual" music as cleansing—like singing bowls or Gregorian chanting. But really ANY music can be cleansing, and it's so much more effective when you use music that you love. Check the time on your washer and build a playlist for the duration it takes to wash your clothes. What kind of vibe do you want to add to your day? What energy do you want to welcome into your space? What music aligns you with that energy?

Turn on your playlist as you start the wash and allow yourself to enjoy the tunes! Maybe you dance around your kitchen or clean another part of your home, and when the playlist ends you know it's time to flip the laundry over. Heck, maybe you have a dryer playlist to introduce even more vibes to your space and make laundry time a deep energetic cleanse of your space and your soul!

Machine drying

Use your dryer balls to set an intention for your clothing while it dries! Grab a wool dryer ball or synthetic alternative and add a few drops of a homemade herb infusion. Use scents that align with the intention you want to invite into your life while you wear the clothes!

Hang drying

This is one of the best ways to deep cleanse not just your clothing but also your space! As your clothes hang dry, set the intention

that any negative energy be cleansed from the space. Feel how the energy shifts as the clothes dry. Once dry, remove the clothes and notice how your space feels!

Folding laundry

Let's tackle that dreaded laundry pile by folding intentions into each garment. Setting intentions in this way is so interesting because your cute little brain acts kind of like a sledding hill. Imagine that one side of the hill every kid in the neighborhood has already gone down. It's like a sheet of ice. You put your sled at the top and you whoosh on down.

But on the other side of the hill is that one path that only a couple of kids have gone down. So you have to use more effort to scoot yourself slowly down the hill.

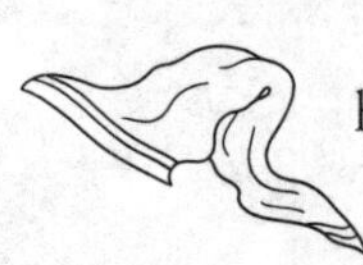

You're already on the fast track of thinking you have a bazillion things you need to do. Thinking you have no time. Thinking you hate this. Thinking laundry's the worst.

However, each time you make the conscious choice to take a deep breath, or notice your feet on the floor, or set an intention as you fold, you're wearing in that new pathway in your brain.

With practice, you can consciously carve new wiring and physically rewire your neural pathways in your brain to see laundry as this opportunity to turn inward and focus on these intentions: *I'm safe. I'm happy. I'm focused.*

Now, the cool part about this sledding hill in your brain is that it doesn't just apply to laundry. How you do anything is how you do everything, remember? The more you practice slowing things down and changing your thoughts around laundry, the more your thoughts will change in the rest of your life.

Here's another meditation to explore.

MEDITATION

Laundry-Folding Enchantment*

*For a guided audio version of this meditation, visit mollydonlan.com/resources.

Bring yourself to that laundry basket and take a deep breath.

Go ahead and pick that basket up, take the laundry to wherever you're planning to fold it, and just dump it out. Really see that pile of clothes, towels, whatever you got going on there. And feel your feet on the floor here. Starting is the hardest part.

Maybe you're thinking, *Oh God, there's so much to do. There's not enough time. I have so many things.* Like a million things buzzing around in your brain. That's okay. Take a breath. Just for this breath, can you let the thoughts go and just feel your feet on the floor?

Now pick up a single item of clothing and imagine you could fold an intention into that article of clothing, so that when you wear it you feel that intention. Maybe it's something like, *I am loved, I am protected, I am happy, I am focused.* Decide for yourself. And as you fold that piece of clothing, repeat that intention to yourself. Either out loud or in your head.

Put that garment to the side. Pick up the next piece of clothing and do the same thing. You could choose one intention for the entire pile or change it up. Maybe your jeans are *May I be grounded*. Perhaps your jackets are *May I be protected*.

Let it be fun. Let it be playful. For the next few minutes, go ahead and fold an intention into each piece of your clothing.

Can you still feel your feet on the floor while you do this? Wiggle your toes if you've lost track of them.

If you feel yourself trying to rush through the task or experiencing again that buzz of like a million things you need to get done, just take one deep breath and let it go. Come back to those intentions. What do you want to feel when you wear that T-shirt, those socks, your favorite pair of underwear?

Fold that intention in.

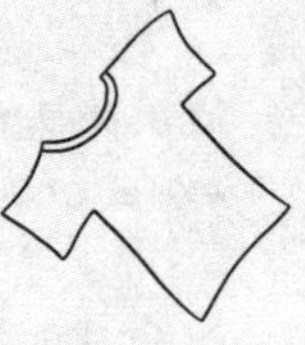

Every so often, take a deep inhale, come back to your feet, clear any stagnant energy out with your exhale.

If you notice your brain popping out of that and going into *I really hate this. It feels like this is taking forever,* consider: First of all, you can stop at any time. But since you've already made some progress, why not keep going? Second of all, let that be okay. Just imagine you could steer that sled off the fast track of thinking into the slow lane of your next intention.

Continue scooting yourself down the hill. One thought at a time, one breath at a time. Keep folding your intentions in.

Notice if you've lost track of your feet; maybe wiggle your toes.

It's really easy to constantly see the mountain ahead of you and not look at the progress you've made. So just for the next couple of breaths, no matter how much laundry you have left to fold, take a moment to recognize and acknowledge the work that you've already done.

Really take in the pile of folded laundry in front of you. Notice it, feel the acknowledgment, the gratitude that you took the time today to do this.

You could have sat around, continued scrolling on your phone, or bought new underwear. But you said, "No, I'm going to take the next few minutes and I'm going to prioritize a few moments of peace, really carving out this Magic moment for myself." And now you have tangible evidence of that choice!

You also may notice the more intangible internal experience of finding a bit more space within yourself.

So just notice: Has anything shifted in your body, your mind, your heart after taking this time?

Maybe something feels different in your space, the energy around you. Just take note.

Perhaps as you fold these last few things, your mouth makes a sort of U shape where the corners turn upward toward your eyes. Maybe your teeth even shine through the space between your lips. Sometimes we call this a *smile*. This might be a foreign experience while you're folding laundry, but just go with it here.

Your brain doesn't know the difference between a real smile and a fake smile. It sends happy hormones through your bloodstream either way. So fake it till you make it—give yourself the biggest, goofiest grin because you did it!

Getting started is the hardest part. So take a moment of gratitude for yourself, for carving out this time, the space, doing something that made you feel supported, maybe a little bit more spacious in the brain. And ultimately, each time you do a practice like this, you carve a path in that sledding hill a little bit more, which becomes easier and easier and easier.

Take one more deep breath in and let a full breath out.

Go ahead and gather any laundry that you haven't folded yet and place it back into the basket or on the chair, wherever it was.

And just take a moment to absorb the effort. Really look at the pile that you did fold. Oftentimes we don't do this. We just take our folded laundry and we shove it in drawers. And then we're like, *Well, I feel like I just did laundry*. So take this marked moment to really land in for yourself. *I did that. I did that.*

What a gift.

Putting away laundry

When putting away your clothes, think about the intentions you've folded into them and the supportive energy as you wear each article of clothing.

Now draw a sigil into your dresser drawer or place a crystal and/or sachet of herbs that corresponds to your intention in your drawer.

As you place each item inside, know that it will marinate in that energy, imbue with that intention, and you will carry that with you throughout the day!

Ironing/steaming clothes

Grab your moon water for this! You're gonna want to fill your steamer or your iron with moon water to begin. Now choose an affirmation that you'd like to infuse into your clothing and your space. Speak the affirmation to the water as it heats up. As you steam your clothing, you'll be spreading that intention throughout your space and into your clothes.

For ironing, you can begin by ironing a sigil into your clothing before smoothing out the wrinkles. Alternatively, you can draw a sigil on your ironing board if you'd like to add the same intention each time—protection sigils work great for this!

Deep Magic

Cleaning the washer

Real quick—what's behind your washer and dryer right now? Dust, lint, a few missing socks, and definitely a whole lot of stagnant energy!

One of the best ways to break yourself out of a funk is to find a pocket of stagnant energy and clear it. So if you've been feeling blah lately or stuck at a crossroads in your life, pull that washer and dryer out and give the space behind it a deep clean with the intention of releasing the energy that's holding you back.

Now, inside the washer is another story—how can we expect the energy of our clothing to be cleansed when the appliance isn't cared for? As you wipe down the inside and outside of your washer, offer gratitude for this machine. Think of all the ways it makes your life easier, all the ways it makes your life better. Think in big and small ways. Without it, where would you be? How would you get your clothes clean? Let that gratitude infuse the machine, so the next time you run a load of laundry your clothes will be infused with this appreciation.

Organizing laundry supplies

The supplies you use for your laundry can influence not just the energy of the clothing but the energy of the person wearing them! There are a few simple ways you can add intention to your laundry supplies. First, choose scents and fragrances that align with the energy you want to carry on your clothing throughout the day. If you use unscented detergent, you can add intention by drawing sigils on the bottles or even by speaking your intention into the washer as you pour in the soap.

Then go through your laundry supplies and purge any that don't align with your intentions or you simply don't like to use. Now wipe down the cabinet or shelf to remove any leftover energy, and place the supplies with reverence. This doesn't need to be fancy! Simply hold your intention for each product in your awareness as you place it into the space. This will not only infuse the product with your energy and Magic, but also help you stay organized in this space!

Decluttering clothes

Who do you want to be one month from now? How about one year from now? Five years? Do the clothes in your closet reflect that version of yourself, or are they holding you back from expanding into your most authentic self? Your clothes are a manifestation tool. When I was burnt out working at nonprofits and trying desperately to get my business off the ground, I used clothing as a tool to propel myself into a completely different life. It was as simple as asking myself, *When I work for myself and my business is thriving, what will I wear each day?* The answer was leggings, a cozy hoodie, a sports bra, and a funny shirt, because it sounded cozy and I felt most myself dressed this way.

When I looked in my closet, I was shocked to find very few of these items! Eighty percent of the clothes in my closet were uncomfortable slacks and button-up blouses. Of course, I couldn't throw my entire wardrobe away, since my office had a dress code. But I slowly decluttered the items I hated wearing at work and replaced them with something closer to my desired outfit. I swapped my uncomfy, ill-fitting bras for sports bras. I got stretchy slacks that felt like leggings, I kept an oversized hoodie in my car to wear on my drive home, and most importantly any moment I was off the clock I was wearing my cozy outfits. Slipping into this outfit made the idea of working for myself feel possible rather than just a daydream.

Who do you want to be? How can you embody that version of yourself in your clothing? Sometimes we think we are living our most authentic selves when in reality we are staying in our comfort zone. Your clothes will reflect who you present yourself as. Keep these questions in mind as you purge your closet and ultimately create space for your manifestations to come to life.

Storing off-season clothing

Need an easy equinox or solstice ritual? Just as you refreshed the home by changing out the decor with the seasons, you can refresh your own personal energy by swapping out your clothing at the turn of the season. Remember that your clothes are the barrier between you and the energy around you that isn't yours. So as you bring in the new season's clothing, give it a spritz of moon water to freshen the energy up.

Mending clothing

In Japan, there's a practice of repairing broken pottery with gold, making the break more visible. This art is called *kintsugi* and it is linked to the Japanese philosophy of wabi-sabi, which encourages us to accept that everything is imperfect and to appreciate imperfections. We'll be using this idea for our Magical practice of mending clothes.

Remember our maxim *How you do anything is how you do everything.* When you practice accepting imperfections in your clothing, you begin to accept imperfections in yourself as well. This can be profoundly healing, leading you to find strength in the journey of becoming who you desire to be—even if you hit pitfalls or aren't where you want to be yet.

Usually we would mend a rip in clothing with a similarly colored thread to the garment. But with the inspiration of kintsugi, you're invited to use a thread that will stand out. You can also look up the Japanese stitching pattern "sashiko" for added inspiration. As you stitch the thread, sit with the idea of wabi-sabi, or explore the following meditation for more inspiration!

MEDITATION

Finding Acceptance

Sit and be however you are. Take a few deep breaths in and notice how your physical body feels in this space.

Notice with curiosity, without judgment, the parts of your body that come into contact with something else. Your feet, your hands, perhaps your legs.

Watch without judgment the sensations in the body: whether they be good, bad, or neutral, see them all through this lens of curiosity.

See the relaxation, the pain, the tension, the softness, all viewed with mere curiosity. Accept all imperfections.

Now become aware of the mind and the thoughts that occupy this space. Once again, notice with curiosity: good, bad, or neutral thoughts are all viewed the same. Accept however your mind is in this moment. Perfectly imperfect.

And now notice the emotional state of your heart, whatever emotions are on the surface or deep below.

However perfectly imperfect you may feel, accepting all emotions just as they are.

Take a deep breath in and let a full breath out.

As you inhale, say to yourself, "I am."

As you exhale, "Perfectly imperfect."

Inhale, "I am."

Exhale, "Acceptance."

Chapter 5

Kitchen

The kitchen, energetically, is the home of our general well-being. Some call it the "heart of the home" to denote how deeply important this area is to our body, mind, and soul. The kitchen is, literally, where we fuel up each day, so energetically it is directly tied to our levels of motivation, health, energy, wealth, and abundance.

Think about the days when your kitchen is a disaster—how much more difficult is it to feed yourself nourishing food? When your kitchen feels clean and organized, you are way more likely to make a healthy meal for you and your family. By tending to the kitchen, you are tending to the health and wellness of your entire being.

"This really really works. I'm a healthy skeptic. I had a hell of a day, and after destroying the kitchen with a soup (witches' brew) and wrestling a threenager to bed, I wanted to curl up with a book or binge-watch something. The pile of dishes was sure to ruin my day tomorrow. So, I turned [the Dishwashing for the Busy Mind meditation, page 137] on reluctantly while my husband showered and I committed to ten minutes. Let me tell you. I was full-on SMILING—smiling, people—while washing up. It's not completely done yet, but I'm so energized I'm going to finish washing up now. I'm so impressed by Mundane Magic. Do yourself a favor and try it. It's truly Magical."

—Alexandra R.

Daily Rituals

Eating three meals a day

We've all been there—whether it's been a nonstop day since your feet hit the floor so you didn't have a chance to whip up some lunch or you've been so hyperfocused on a project you just plain forgot to eat, three P.M. hits and you feel like crap because you haven't eaten in hours.

You go to open the fridge and all you see are ingredients, so you pace between the pantry and fridge over and over until you get so frustrated you give up and don't eat anything at all. After spiraling the rest of the day, you're teetering on the edge of a temper tantrum until dinner.

Consider WHY you are skipping meals. Is it because you don't want to put in the effort to cook? Or maybe you simply don't know WHAT to eat? We'll fix both issues with Magic.

Problem: "I don't want to cook"
Solution: Low-effort meal spells

By adding intention to the cooking process, you turn a drab hyperfixation meal into an abundance ritual, or a boring piece of toast into a clear communication spell. There are several super easy recipe spells in the appendix of this book that literally anyone can make (page 309). (As someone who could burn spaghetti, I promise these are ACTUALLY easy!) But you can also make ANY meal into a spell. Here are two ways to get started:

START WITH THE INTENTION

This is great if you don't want to cook, because it helps you create a bit of novelty around the process of cooking and eating. Decide what intention you want the spell to support you with: abundance, healing, peace, focus, creativity.

Now use the spells in the appendix OR simply use your intuition as a guide to pull you in the direction of an ingredient you have on hand that supports your intention. Reminder: YOU ARE THE MAGIC! Don't overthink this. If cauliflower feels healing to you, go for it. You don't need my permission or anyone else's!

Now that you have your first ingredient, decide again, using the same process, what ingredients will help you round out the intention. Make sure you choose foods that you'd actually want to eat together—for instance, brown sugar and cinnamon for luck, onions and garlic for banishing, corn and beans for prosperity, you get the idea.

Let your intuition lead the way. Maybe you throw things together and make your own recipe, or maybe these two ingredients have sparked a recipe idea for you to research in your favorite cookbook. As you add more ingredients, give them a job by stating your intention for using them! Let it be fun, creative, inspiring. You can't do this wrong.

Start with the Recipe

This is great if you know what you're craving but don't feel motivated to make it. Research the Magical properties of the ingredients in your recipe—again, you can either use the appendix of this book or your own intuition. What emotions and associations do YOU hold for each ingredient? Start to build your spell based on the intentions that resonate with you, and let this fuel your motivation.

As you make your meal, give each ingredient a job by stating its intention to yourself. Not everything needs a complex intention—I once added sprinkles to a latte spell because they were fun!

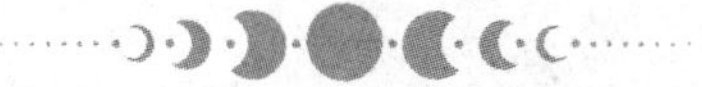

Spicy Omelet for Task Initiation and Motivation

Try this simple and quick recipe infused with intention; you can find a few more simply Magical recipes in the appendix.

INGREDIENTS:

- **2 to 3 eggs** *for creativity and birthing new ideas*
- **Pinch of salt** *for protection*
- **Crack of black pepper** *to banish lethargy*
- *To taste:* **sliced jalapeños** *to grow your motivation*
- *To taste:* **nutritional yeast** *or* **cheddar cheese** *for creativity and abundance*

INSTRUCTIONS:

- Mix all ingredients together and add to a hot nonstick pan. Cook on low-medium heat until the bottom solidifies. Flip carefully and let cook for one more minute. Fold and serve immediately.

Problem: "I don't know what to eat"
Solution: Deciding-what-to-eat spell jar

This fun and tactile tutorial will help you in the moment and whenever you feel stuck deciding what to eat in the future!

Grab a small jar (an old spice container or pill bottle works great!) and toss in a pinch of the following ingredients. Remember: use what you have—if you don't have something listed, use the Ingredients by Intention section of the appendix (page 301) to find a substitute:

- Lavender to relax the mind
- Mint to bring mental clarity
- Clove for focus
- Salt for protection
- Tiger's-eye for decision making

Seal your spell jar with yellow candle wax for confidence and energy, then top with a sigil or affirmation that supports you having clarity around what to eat. Keep this in your kitchen and shake whenever you feel like you're opening and closing the fridge too many times!

The spell jar will bring your awareness back to mindful intention—remember that freeze response? Your brain might be so hungry it thinks there's a tiger afoot, impacting your ability to make rational decisions like what to eat. By shaking the spell jar, you're short-circuiting that tiger response, coming back to the present moment, and reminding yourself to take a deep breath. This helps your brain come out of that freeze response and grab a bite to eat without the constant back-and-forth from fridge to pantry.

Grocery shopping

Grocery shopping is the perfect opportunity to strengthen your intuition! Often we struggle to trust our intuition because we place a ton of pressure on the answers we're receiving. Imagine if you had a friend who you only ever talked to when you needed life-altering advice, like: Where should I move? Should I date this person? Should I quit my job and sell shirts for a traveling punk rock band that claims they will one day make it big? You would be less likely to take that friend's advice than, say, the friend who you talk to every day about mundane things.

Treat your intuition like a friend. As you make your grocery list, ask your intuition: Do I want pizza or pasta? Notice how the answer comes through. Remember: your intuition can come up in different ways. Let's explore a few.

PSYCHIC SENSES: TYPE OF INTUITIVE MESSAGE	HOW IT SHOWS UP	. . . AT THE GROCERY STORE
Clairvoyance: Clear seeing	**Visually:** In dreams or meditation; may be seen as an image or color or shape.	You find yourself dreaming about food, visualizing the food you want, being drawn to a certain color on the packaging.
Claircognizance: Clear knowing	**Gut instinct:** Something pops into your head; you don't know how you know it, but you just do.	You get a craving for pasta; you turn down an aisle because you have a hunch that you'll find something good.
Clairsentience: Clear feeling	**Sensation and emotion:** You experience physical sensations in the body or you experience an emotion.	Your stomach gurgles when you think about a food; you feel excited when you consider a recipe.
Clairaudience: Clear hearing	**Auditory:** You hear sounds, songs, or noises that cue you to the answer.	The lyrics of the song playing in your head steer you toward a food item; your hearing gets clearer or more vivid as you approach an aisle.
Clairgustance: Clear tasting	**Taste:** You crave or tangibly taste a flavor.	Your mouth waters at the idea of different foods; you crave certain tastes like sweet or sour.

As you go through your grocery list, explore the different layers of your intuition. How do you know that's what you want to eat? Then, when you're at the grocery store, use your psychic senses to help you decide on ingredients. Hold up two different boxes of pasta: Which one visually appeals to you more? How does your body respond to the two logos? What's playing on the radio when you determine which one you'll buy? Practicing this will strengthen your intuition in the long run and turn grocery shopping into a more mindful experience.

Drinking water

Water responds to intention. We have Dr. Masaru Emoto to thank for the research on this. So what better way to infuse your entire day with Magic than through your water.

The obvious idea here would be to drink moon water. One of my Instagram followers messaged me a picture once where she had put a case of water outside under the full moon and I thought that was GENIUS. I won't lie to you—I forget to put my water out under the moon more often than I remember. Fortunately, there are other ways you can add Magic to your water that don't require you to plan ahead.

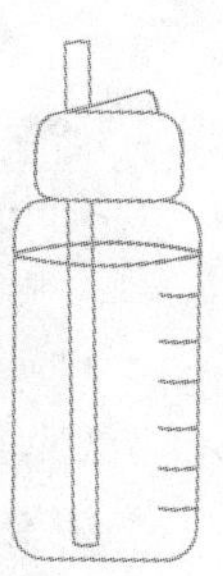

Decide what intention you'd like to infuse in your water throughout the day. What do you want to integrate on a cellular level, in your water, your day, or your life?

You can simply write that intention on your water bottle, but Sticker Magic is also great for this. Decorate your bottle with stickers that symbolize your intention, or write the intention on the outside of the bottle in clear nail polish if you want to be more subtle. You could even make a sigil for that intention and draw it on the bottle or the cap so you see it before taking a drink. This brings new meaning to the phrase *emotional-support water bottle.*

Crystal water infusions are a powerful tool for bringing Magic to the otherwise boring task of staying hydrated. However, do NOT place the crystals directly in your water. I don't even recommend those water bottles with crystals in them unless there is a separate compartment so the crystal never touches the water. As I discuss in the ritual bath section (see page 154), some crystals can deteriorate in water while others can leach toxins that you shouldn't drink. Even if your crystal is water-safe, it is likely covered in a polish that is not food-grade. It is safest to avoid placing crystals in water you are going to drink and instead opt for this indirect method of infusing water with crystal energy:

Safely infusing water with crystal energy

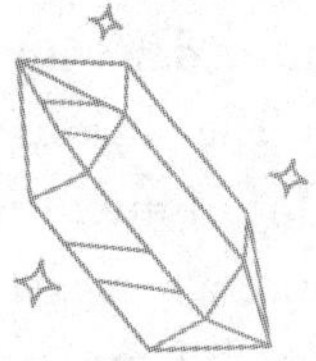

- Grab four clear quartz points and whatever crystal you want to infuse your water with.
- Place the water in the center of your table. (Note: It can be in ANY container, open or closed, glass or plastic—it does not matter.)
- Set the clear quartz points around the container holding the water so that the pointed ends are closest to the container.
- Now, on the outside of the quartz points, opposite the water, place the crystal you want to infuse your water with. The crystal can be any size and shape for this.
- The quartz points act like a slingshot, directing the energy of the crystal into the water.

- Let it sit overnight, or use Reiki to infuse the energy into your water faster.

Cleaning water bottles

Did you know that your water bottle collects more bacteria in a week than a dog's water dish? Sorry, that fact ruined my life and now I need you to know it, too. If your water bottle is filled with that much bacteria, think about how much stagnant energy it has picked up! Everywhere your bottle has gone with you, everyone it's been around—it's picking up energy from all of it. No wonder you feel stuck or stagnant! Let's clear that energy and clean out the bacteria.

Grab a dish soap and a bottle brush. As you scrub the inside of the bottle, imagine all that energy loosening up with the suds. Shake the soapy water inside to collect any remaining energy and drain it down the sink. Before rinsing, make sure you get the outside of the bottle, too!

Now, the mouthpiece is important to cleanse because it is the part most in contact with your voice. As you clean this part of the bottle, set the intention that your words be loving and kind—especially to yourself.

Finally, fill your water bottle up and speak your intention for the day into your water. Each time you fill it, use that moment as a reminder to come back to your intention.

Feeding your pet and washing pet bowls

Washing your pet's food and water bowls is important to keep them healthy and happy, but it can be easy to overlook! One way to manage this is by letting your pet's feeding time become a mindful moment for you. Place a fresh bowl of food down, and while they are eating, stop and take a few deep breaths or stretch your body. Perhaps you take this time to do a mini meditation, scanning your body and noticing any sensations that may be present. When your pet has finished eating, pick up the bowl and wash it or set it in the dishwasher. Notice how you feel after pausing for this time.

We know our pets aren't always perfect angels, but it's not their fault they pooped on the floor or tore up your favorite paperback! As you wash their water dish, rinse the slate clean energetically, forgive them for their missteps, and clear away that energy. When you fill their water bowl, consider speaking words of affirmation and gratitude into their water. If you have an anxious pet, perhaps you'll speak words like, "Calm, peace"; if you have a barking dog, perhaps you'll say, "Quiet, hushed"; if you have a cat that hisses at your friends when they come over, maybe try, "Kind, nice, polite."

Tea Magic

Tea presents so many Magical opportunities! For the purpose of this book, let's explore two: Magical correspondences and tea meditation.

When choosing a tea blend, you can decide based on the Magical correspondences of the ingredients. Similarly to how we conducted a simple meal spell (on page 117), you can start with the tea you're in the mood for and research the Magical properties of the blend, or you can start with your intention and choose a blend based on that. This is a great opportunity to incorporate a full-blown ritual into your day, especially when paired with meditation!

Meditation is just about paying attention to what's happening while it's happening. We can do that with our eyes and watch the little bubbles in our teakettle boil. We can do that with our ears and listen to the sounds of the kettle whistling. We can do that with our nose as we smell the aroma of the tea. And we can definitely do that with the taste of our favorite tea.

One of my favorite tools for meditation is to Pavlov yourself to meditate. This means to build an association between a specific sensory experience—such as the scent of your fave perfume or the sound of birds chirping—and the experience of meditation. Making tea is a perfect time to try this out.

If you have a teakettle that makes a sound like a beep or whistle, just take a deep breath every time you hear it for the next couple of days.

You can do this with the flavor and scent of your favorite cuppa using the following meditation. Repeat this practice as often as you can, and then eventually it's going to become automatic. You will open your fave tea bag and suddenly feel a sense of gratitude, calm, and presence. It's true Magic in all forms!

MEDITATION

Steeping with Gratitude

While you fill your kettle, be intentional about even these most basic steps. Maybe you make a cup of tea every day. But can you do it with awareness?

How do the buttons of your kettle feel underneath your thumb? Can you see the water and watch it just softly ebb and flow until it settles down? See the gentle waves in the water, the little bubbles. Just use your eyes to tune in to that.

Take a couple of deep breaths. While the water is heating up, think of three things that you're grateful for. Just let yourself sit with that gratitude—steep in the gratitude, if you will—while the water heats up.

And while you're sitting with those three examples of gratitude, maybe you close your eyes and just let yourself listen to the kettle.

As you slow down this small part of your day, notice: How do your body and mind respond to that? Maybe your brain feels like you slammed on the brakes on the highway, all the stuff from the backseat flies forward, and your brain feels really busy. That's okay.

What happens if you just let the dust settle?

Almost like when you shake up a snow globe and then let it sit. The more you can tune in to the tea-making sounds, that gratitude, the more you might notice the brain starts to quiet down.

When you hear the kettle go off, take a deep breath.

Now take your tea and take a big whiff. It smells so good. Savor that scent.

As you put the tea into your teacup, see if you can really tune in to what you're doing while you're doing it. Feel the kettle in your hand, watch the steam, listen to the sounds of the water pouring over the tea.

And while the tea is steeping, set a timer for however long it needs to steep. Now hover your hands around the cup. Close your eyes and let yourself tune in to that feeling of the heat coming off the cup.

Bring your hands as close as you need to without touching it until you feel that heat.

And then you can play a little bit. What happens if you bring your hands a little bit further out? How far can you bring your hands while still feeling that heat?

Let your shoulders relax and then bring your hands a little closer. Maybe you feel the heat becoming more intense. Just use sensation, heat in the hands, to anchor your awareness here.

And then maybe you bring your hands further out to see if you can still feel that heat. One more time—bring them back in a little closer.

Call back into your awareness those three things that you're grateful for. Maybe there are three new things now. Imagine you could take that energy of gratitude, sending it from your heart, down your hands, out the palms, into your tea. As if you're infusing the water, the tea leaves, with that gratitude.

Now extend that gratitude to the tea itself, feeling grateful for the person who blended it, who packaged it, who put it on the shelf of the store that you got it from. All the different hands that these ingredients had to pass through before they got to you.

Can you find gratitude for each of those people, each of those ingredients, maybe even the earth itself? And then see if you can still feel the heat of the tea in your hands.

Now bring your hands to your heart space and take a moment of gratitude for yourself, for taking the time to slow down. For taking this time to enjoy and appreciate this tea, to enjoy and appreciate this life, one sip at a time.

Finally, the tea has steeped. Bring all the senses into your experience before you take that first sip of tea. So maybe you feel the heat once more, and then pick your teacup up and really look at the colors, watching the petals or the tea flowers, whatever your tea is made of, unfurling, blooming. Smell the aroma.

And take one sip with gratitude. Smile and enjoy.

Coffee Magic

Coffee as a Magical ingredient helps speed things up—think of how the cartoon character always moves faster after a cup of coffee, or how our bowels move faster after that first morning cup. So we can use coffee in any spell that we want to make happen quickly OR we can make a cup of coffee into a spell.

If you add milk, cream, sweetener, or flavored syrups to your coffee, you can choose them based on intentions. Then hold those intentions in your awareness as you pour the ingredients into your cup. Stir everything together with a sigil and you have a super easy morning ritual!

Here are a few ideas to get started. You'll also find some fun Magical coffee syrup recipes in the appendix of this book (page 313).

CREAM AND SWEETENER OPTIONS	MAGICAL INTENTIONS
Dairy milk *(including half-and-half and whipped cream)*	Abundance, prosperity, healing, beauty
Oat milk	Healing, abundance, perseverance, new beginnings, family
Coconut *(including coconut milk and coconut sugar)*	Purification, protection
Almond milk	Banishing, luck, prosperity, love, energy
Cashew milk	Abundance, prosperity, communication

CREAM AND SWEETENER OPTIONS	MAGICAL INTENTIONS
Soy milk	Luck, inspiration, communication, creativity
Macadamia nut milk	Love, abundance, protection, healing
Pistachio milk	Generosity, patience
Hazelnut milk	Wisdom, nourishment, manifestation
Sugar	Sweetness, love, attraction, cleansing
Brown sugar	Comfort, love, attraction
Date sugar	Spirituality, rebirth, love
Molasses	Energy, balancing, motivation, cleansing
Agave	Passion, transformation, abundance, health
Honey	Sweetness, love, blessings, spirituality, healing, motivation
Maple	Longevity, protection, sweetness, growth, balance, tolerance, intelligence
Mocha	Friendship, self-love, grounding, prosperity, happiness, positive energy
Marshmallow	Love, protection, cleansing, luck, healing
Stevia	Cleansing, protection, clarity

CREAM AND SWEETENER OPTIONS	MAGICAL INTENTIONS
Monk fruit	Longevity, healing, clarity
Cinnamon*	Abundance, luck, prosperity, protection
Salt**	Protection, cleansing, purification

** Cinnamon is hydrophobic, meaning it won't mix into your coffee directly. For best results, add a pinch to your coffee grounds before brewing.*

*** Don't knock it till you try it! Add a pinch of salt to your coffee grounds to cut the acidity.*

Simmer pots

Simmer pots are a great place to start when it comes to cleaning the kitchen while cleansing and deodorizing your home. Simmer pots are simple, easy, and highly motivating. They make your space smell amazing without using any harsh fragrances or chemicals, and you can mix and match ingredients based on your intentions and what you have on hand. Here are some ideas to get you started, but also check the appendix of this book for a list of simmer pot recipes by intention (page 315).

- **Use food scraps:** Orange peels, lemon peels, apple cores, used tea bags, pumpkin rinds, and flower petals all make great ingredients for simmer pots. You don't need to use fresh produce every time—if you're on a clementine kick, throw those peels in a simmer pot!

- **Freeze ingredients:** If you have an abundance of oranges that are about to go bad, slice them up and freeze them for your simmer pots. Freezing also works great for food scraps or loose-leaf tea that has already been steeped.

- **Use expired ingredients:** Simmer pots are a great way to use expired spices or fruit that is about to turn.

To make a simmer pot, fill a pot ¾ of the way full with water and set it on the stove. Add whatever ingredients you like, stating their intention as you add them in. Once your simmer pot is complete, turn the stove up to high until the water bubbles, then drop it down to low and let it simmer. Set a timer and check it every so often to ensure the water hasn't evaporated, adding more as needed.

You can make a short-term simmer pot while you clean the kitchen, or have it going all week by adding more water to it. Once the ingredients have run their course, compost or throw them away and say thank you for their support. You can strain the water and use it in other ways. Add the water to a spray bottle of witch hazel to make a room spray, or add a splash of the water to your mop water to infuse the intention throughout the rest of your space.

Garbage disposal

If you're lucky enough to have a garbage disposal in your kitchen sink, this is a great opportunity to reuse an old simmer pot. Remove any cinnamon sticks and large chunks of citrus from your pot after it's simmered on the stove for some time. Dump the remaining water, herbs, and sliced citrus down the garbage disposal with the intention of cleansing the pipes. Add a handful of ice cubes and turn on the faucet. As the disposal chops up the ice and fruit, the simmer pot's scent and intention will fill your space and clear the energy of your sink.

Magical Upkeep

Taking out the trash

Motivate yourself to take out the trash by using it as a tool to connect with your spirit team. Your spirit team is a collection of energetic beings who support you every day—think of them like guardian angels or a collection of advisors. Some may be ancestors or deities; some may be more nebulous like the elements—water, earth, air, fire, spirit—or energetic blobs.

Think of this—if you were having family over to chat, you wouldn't want your full trash can stinking up the house, right? So, use taking out the trash as a way of initiating the connection to your spirit team and offering them your respect.

As you take out the trash, set the intention that any negative entities or unhealed beings leave your energetic space. As you set the new bin liner in place, invite your spirit team to connect with you.

Sit down in a comfortable space and breathe gently in and out. Set a timer and become curious about whoever from your spirit team connects and however they arrive to your awareness. Sometimes they may appear visibly as shadows out of the corner of your eyes or as images in your mind. They may also show up as an inner knowing, like you just become aware of their presence, or a song may play in your head, or you may feel chills or goose bumps. Get curious about what you notice. Have a conversation with them—ask them how they support you, what they like, how they would like to be contacted, etc. Do this often to strengthen your connection to your team!

Going to the dump or recycling center

As you look over your trash and recycling that has piled up, notice how your space feels. Because how you do anything is how you do everything, you're not just getting rid of these boxes; you are also creating space for fresh energy to come in. This can help reduce tension in the mind and the body, and even reduce negative thought patterns. Energetic obstacles that are holding you back accumulate energetically on this stuff. Release them as you bring your trash to the dump or your recyclables to the recycling center. Afterward, appreciate all the space and fresh energy you now have.

Doing the dishes

Washing the dishes consistently ranks in the top three most requested chores to transform through Mundane Magic—and for good reason. This task is seemingly never-ending, feels daunting, and literally piles up. But with the right mindset and a little bit of intention, the dishes can be transformed from something you dread to something that actually helps you feel more grounded and at ease. Try this meditation next time you do the dishes and see for yourself.

MEDITATION

Dishwashing for the Busy Mind*

*For a guided audio version of this meditation, visit mollydonlan.com/resources.

Put your feet on the floor and walk over to your pile of dishes. That's it. That's step number one, sometimes the hardest step. The invitation is to just do what you can in ten minutes.

You don't have to complete the task. You don't have to have a completely clean kitchen. This is just about making it more manageable for right now.

As you stand in front of your sink, feel your feet on the floor and the support of the earth beneath you, grounding your awareness into your body.

Anytime you bring awareness down into your feet, you drop out of the worried thinking mind. So you're invited to keep this connection to your feet. And anytime your awareness floats up into your mind, just come back down.

Maybe even wiggle your toes. And now turn on the water. Notice the sounds that it makes.

If you're someone who fills the sink, you can do that now. Or if you're someone who rinses the dishes before soaping them, do that now.

One way or another, run your hand under the water, and just feel the sensation of the temperature.

Now pick up your sponge. Feel the sensation, the textures, the temperature of the sponge as you run it under the water.

As you add the soap, see if you can smell if there's a scent to the soap, or maybe there's another smell lingering. Good or bad or neutral.

Just coming into the senses brings us into the present moment.

Now grab your first dish. As you hold that dish in your hand and start to scrub it with the sponge, imagine you could slough off any stagnant energy. Energy not just being held on the dish, but being collected in your space.

And because you still have your feet on the floor, any stagnant energy that's within you is flowing out of your feet into the earth. As you rinse that dish, see it as a visual reminder that, with each exhale, you're rinsing your energy field, clearing out the energy you may have picked up from other people or places that you've been.

Continue to feel the energy slough off with the sponge and see the soap go down the drain as a visual reminder that you're releasing that energy into the earth.

If your brain feels really busy, that's okay. Just wiggle your toes, come back down out of the head into the body.

Maybe tune back in to the temperature of the water or the feeling of the sponge in your hands or the smell of the soap. Use your senses to come out of your mind rather than judging your mind for doing its job.

Thinking is literally what it's been designed and programmed to do. And we want it to think, we need it to think. It's what's kept you alive so far. So when your brain is really busy, it's actually a really compassionate response. There's a part of your brain that's like, *I'm not so sure about this.*

Wiggling your toes, coming into your senses, taking a deep breath is like telling your brain, *I've got this. I've got this. We're good right now.*

See if you can feel that for the next couple of dishes that you clean, staying kind to yourself, kind to your brain, no matter how busy it might be.

And now you may still have a lot of dishes to do. That's okay. Notice your progress so far, whether you've cleaned one dish or a whole rackful of them. Getting started was the hardest part.

So take a moment now as we pass this halfway mark to pat yourself on the back. You did that. You got through the hardest part. You started the engine.

Can you find a sense of gratitude for yourself for taking this time? Acknowledging that you could have continued scrolling on your phone or ordered takeout, used a paper towel instead of a plate. You've said, "No, just for this breath, just for this pocket of time, I'm going to give myself the gift of a more functional kitchen, but not a perfect one."

By doing this meditation, you've created more space in the mind, the energy body, to have a more functional inner experience. Again, you may not feel perfect. We're not striving for perfection.

Once again, feel your feet on the floor. Take those deep breaths in.

Let the soapy water be a reminder that you're shedding other people's energy with each exhale, purifying your energy.

Now, as you breathe in, call your energy back from wherever you may have left it behind throughout your day, your week, your month. Call it back purified by the water. Feel your energy come back just with that intention.

Come back to your body. Cleansed, renewed. And just as water can grow a garden, that energy can grow your awareness, your kindness, your compassionate sense of self, your patience, your motivation, your momentum for whatever you need to do with the rest of your day.

As you look to the stack of dishes you've already cleaned, no matter how many there are left to do, see those as a representation of this time that you took for yourself. Time to recharge, replenish, call your energy back, to set an energetic boundary with other people's energy.

Take a couple of breaths and notice how you feel. Has anything changed in your body, your mind, your heart?

Remember: your intention when you started was to just use this pocket of time to create a more functional space. You did that. Whether you washed one dish or all of them, you did that. So you can stop here, but if you feel like you've gathered some momentum and it feels good to keep going, allow yourself to do so. But know that you have a choice.

You're in the driver's seat here. Whatever you're deciding, take a deep breath in. Open your mouth and let it go.

Wiggle your toes, feel your feet on the floor, roll your shoulders. Maybe rock your head side to side.

Give yourself a pat on the back for completing this practice.

Emptying and loading the dishwasher

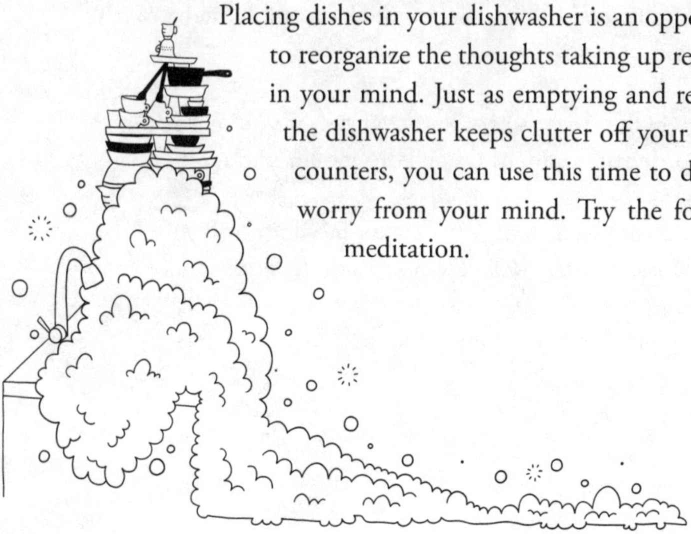

Placing dishes in your dishwasher is an opportunity to reorganize the thoughts taking up real estate in your mind. Just as emptying and reloading the dishwasher keeps clutter off your kitchen counters, you can use this time to declutter worry from your mind. Try the following meditation.

MEDITATION

Emptying Your Mind of Worry

Open the dishwasher and open your awareness to that thing your brain has been worrying about all day. Let yourself see this worry for all it is: Where does it come from? What is fueling it?

As you unload the dishes, allow your brain to think through this worry. What's the fear underneath it? What does your brain assume about this situation? How likely is that to happen? Are there any possible solutions you haven't considered yet?

Breathe deeply into your abdomen as you explore this worry, letting your brain marinate on it. Knowing you can always release the worry if it feels too intense.

Once the dishes are unloaded, it's time to shift into solutions. As you load the dirty dishes into the machine, consider all possible angles of this situation. How would you handle that hypothetical worst-case scenario? What support can you call in, whether that's energetic support or physical support like finances or emotional support like community? Are there people in your life who you can call on to help you through this?

With each dish you add to the dishwasher, consider thinking of a new solution to this potential worry. Don't limit yourself to what feels "possible" or "likely"—your anxiety isn't worried about the likeliness of the worry, so don't limit your solution brain as you come up with these ideas.

Finally, load the detergent into the dishwasher with the intention to wash this worry away from your mind, replacing it with the ease that you know you've got this!

Wash the worry off your hands with soap and water, and release the solutions into the universe. Take an inhale and say to yourself, "Just for this breath." And as you exhale say to yourself, "I will not worry." Repeat as many times as you need.

Tidying the kitchen

Keeping the kitchen tidy in between meals is a great way to prioritize your well-being and health. Where your awareness goes, energy flows, so by tidying your kitchen you're bringing attention to your health and the well-being of your entire family.

Cleaning the counters

Use moon water and soap to scrub your countertops. Rub in counterclockwise motions to banish any stagnant or stuck energy from the space; rub in clockwise motions to invite health and wellness into the space. To add even more Magic into this task, choose a scented counter spray that aligns with the intention you wish to call into your space.

Setting the table

As you set the table for your family, reflect on gratitude. Beginning at your own place setting, as you place each utensil, dish, cup, and napkin, offer a statement of gratitude to yourself. Now move on to the next place setting and do the same thing for that family member. Continue until the table is set. This is a great chore to get kids involved with or to do before a family gathering to promote peace and harmony within the space!

Decluttering mugs, reusable containers, and under the sink

Keeping clutter out of the kitchen is easier said than done, until we remember the energetic intention of this space: to prioritize your and your family's health and well-being. As you approach your space, ask yourself, *Does this item contribute to my well-being or detract from it?* Doing this will bring clarity to your intention and strengthen this resolve in your space.

Crumbs in the silverware drawer

How those crumbs end up in the silverware drawer is one Magic trick I don't have the answer to. But you can use those little crumbs as an opportunity to purge the little obstacles that show up in your path. You know those little things you don't pay attention to but come back to bite you in the long term? As you vacuum these crumbs up, think of it like bringing awareness to those other little things—what are they? What comes to mind? And as you vacuum them away, set the intention to release them from your mind and body.

Feeding pets

If you feed your pets fresh food and treats, consider infusing these with the energy based on their Magical correspondences. There's a whole list in the Ingredients Appendix (page 291), but here are some ideas to get you started:

TREAT	MAGICAL CORRESPONDENCES
Yogurt drops	Creativity, mood lifting
Salt licks	Protection, cleansing
Birdseed	Love, growth, expansion
Lettuce	Protection, grounding, sleep
Carrots	Passion, creativity, grounding, abundance

TREAT	MAGICAL CORRESPONDENCES
Crickets	Self-expression, intuition, luck
Worms	Luck, resilience, replenishment
Mice	Courage, resourcefulness, wit
Bananas	Abundance, resilience
Strawberries	Luck, self-love, dedication
Shrimp	Joy, fortune, longevity

Deep Magic

Organizing the fridge

This is a fantastic new moon ritual. As you consider what you want to manifest and invite into your life over the next moon cycle, now is the perfect time to take action toward your goals. The simplest moments of your day, like eating a meal, can be powerful accelerators for manifestations. As you go through your fridge, release (throw away or compost) anything that is expired or that you don't like. These items energetically create stagnation, but they also clutter up your fridge, preventing you from finding what you do like.

Grab an erasable marker and draw sigils on your leftover containers. Maybe you create a sigil for good health or focus or nourishment. While you're at it, add the date you put the food away so you know when it's time to toss it or eat it.

Finally, give a good scrub-down of your fridge with moon water! Add it to your soap or leave your spray bottle of cleaner on the windowsill overnight to infuse the entire bottle. As you clean the gunk away from your fridge, you're clearing the energy of your food.

Cleaning the oven

In feng shui, keeping the oven clean promotes a good flow of energy and abundance. Using the Magical properties of different cleaning agents, you can amplify this flow of energy and invite even more abundance into your home.

Begin by making a paste out of baking soda and water. Baking soda, energetically, can be used for cleansing and banishing. So as you spread the paste within your oven, allow it to loosen both stuck food and stuck energy from your home. Let the paste sit while you soak the oven racks in dish soap and water, adding a splash of moon water or a crack of salt to increase the energetic cleansing.

Now add some white vinegar to a spray bottle—vinegar is great for preventing unwanted energetic attachments from forming. Spritz the vinegar over the baking soda mixture and begin scrubbing, rinsing away the residue.

Finally, fill a loaf pan with water and add one tablespoon of coffee and one tablespoon of vanilla extract for soothing and healing your space. Place the loaf pan on the center rack of your oven and bake at 300°F (150°C) to infuse your space with the scent and intention. Keep it there until the scent infuses into your space, and refill as needed—don't let it completely dry out or it will burn!

Cleaning cupboards: insides, outsides, and tops

Leave your favorite multipurpose spray on the windowsill overnight to infuse it with the energy of the moon. Now draw a sigil for health on the outside of the bottle before cleaning your cupboards. Be sure to do the inside and the outside of the doors, as well as dusting the tops of the cupboards and their doors. Finish by cleaning off the handles. This is a great task to do with the equinoxes and solstices to initiate that shift in energy for your whole space.

Descaling the coffee machine or teakettle

This is a great full moon task. Combine water, a splash of lemon juice for cleansing, and a splash of vinegar to offer protection to your teakettle or coffee machine. Run the coffee machine cycle through or boil the kettle to infuse them with those intentions. Finally, rinse the device clean and run regular water through the cycle one more time to ensure all the vinegar is out. End by making yourself a cup of tea or coffee to celebrate yourself with some Little Treat Magic!

Organizing spices and herbs

Going through your spice drawer is the perfect starting place for a kitchen witch! Before you buy any fancy herbs or ingredients for your simmer pots, spell jars, or ritual baths, get clear on what you already have.

Pull out your spices and flip this book open to the Ingredients by Intention list in the appendix (page 301). Look up each ingredient and label it with the Magic intentions listed there. For spice blends, you can look up the individual herbs and spices in the blend to find each one's intentions. Now you can sort items by intention or make a table of what you have and all the intentions that are covered by the items in your spice drawer.

If you find any expired spices, grab these and use them in your spells first! You can toss them in a simmer pot or a spell jar or even in your money bowl (see page 223), depending on what herb it is. Now that you have an empty jar, you can clean it out and use it for a spell jar itself!

Now, when you grab spices for a recipe, you can easily add an intention to your dish by stating the intention you wrote down on the jars.

Cleaning the microwave

Grab a mug and fill it with half a cup of water, a slice of lemon, and one or two teaspoons of vanilla extract. Lemon helps cleanse the energy of your space while removing stuck food from your microwave; vanilla adds a sweet scent to the space and soothes the energy of your space. Microwave on high for thirty to sixty seconds. While you wait, take this time to shake out energy from your body: explore shaking your right leg, then your left, before shaking out each arm.

Once the steam from the mug has loosened the gunk from your microwave, use a cloth dampened with moon water to wipe down the inside.

Chapter 6

Bathroom

Your bathroom is associated with the element of water, which can energetically influence the abundance in your space as well as your emotional resilience. When we consider the water element, the word *flow* comes to mind. By caring for your bathroom, you're caring for the flow of your prosperity. This is a great space to pay attention to if you're manifesting more money or a new career opportunity into your life. If finances feel tight, try deep cleaning this space to allow the energy of money to flow more easily.

As far as emotional resilience goes, I like to compare it to the waves in the ocean. Imagine you're standing waist-deep in the ocean. You have two options: you can become very rigid and likely get knocked over by the next wave, or you can stay loose and stay afloat. This is how we relate to our emotions as well. If you are experiencing emotions that seem to take over and disrupt your day-to-day life, try cleaning one area of your bathroom while breathing into your abdomen. This can help improve your ability to flow with your emotions and, as you cleanse the space, release any stagnant energy that may be contributing to that emotional rigidity. Let's explore some more Magical ways to keep the energy of your bathroom in flow.

> "Thinking about how the bathroom holds a lot of stagnant outside energy has really helped with getting my shower and toilet scrubbed down more often. I now SEE and recognize that energy and want to cleanse it, rather than seeing a chore. I'm just starting to incorporate moon water and scents to boost the cleanse more!"
>
> —Kels

Daily Rituals

Brushing your teeth and flossing

Did you know your brain creates new neural pathways *FASTER* when you introduce an element of play? Try it for yourself. While you floss your teeth, say your favorite affirmations out loud. It's going to sound garbled and silly, but that's exactly the point! While you're at it, turn your bathroom into a vision board. If you're staring into the mirror, why not decorate it with sticky notes of positive affirmations or things you wish to manifest into your life?

Brushing your teeth is the perfect opportunity to practice two minutes of meditation or Reiki, focusing on the feeling of your feet on the ground or the taste of the toothpaste in your mouth. Let yourself be fully immersed in the present moment, then rinse and go about your day!

Finally, before you swish your mouth with water or mouthwash, state your intention for the day out loud. Water responds to words and intentions, so this is a great opportunity to bookend your day with your intention in your morning and evening routines.

Bathing, showering, and washing your hair

Love it or hate it, you need to bathe from time to time. Maybe you're someone who avoids it at all costs or someone like me who struggles to get in the shower but once you do you don't want to leave. Either way, bathing is one of the best ways to cleanse your energy and feel more mentally focused, clear, and motivated for alllll the other tasks on your to-do list. Here's how you can make it even more Magical.

Any product you use for the shower can have a Magical intention infused in it. For example, if your shampoo has rosemary in it, congratulations—you now have a hair wash that will protect your energy. Sea-salt body scrub? Great for cleansing and protection as well. Lavender body wash? Great for peace and relaxation. Look up the ingredients in your favorite bath products and write their Magical correspondences on the label. You can also create sigils for other intentions you want to bring into your day and draw them on the bottle. Say you want to shower before bed—

you can carve into your bar of soap a sigil to help you sleep. Want more energy in the morning after you shower? Draw a motivation sigil on the bottom of your citrus-scented body wash.

Now, washing your hair might be a different story. You may be okay with showering but put your hair-washing routine off as long as possible. This is a great opportunity for a DEEEEEP energy cleanse of your chakras—as you scrub the shampoo into your hair, meditate on the energy of the crown being completely cleared. As the shampoo runs off your head in the water, imagine or visualize the shampoo clearing all the energy centers down your body before it runs down the drain.

Now let's talk ritual baths—these are such a powerful tool for cleansing and for literally swimming in your intentions. A ritual bath can be as elaborate or simple as you want. You can use a number of ingredients, but here are a few best practices to make sure you don't make an even BIGGER mess during your bath.

If you're adding herbs to your bath, first things first, make sure they're not going to irritate your skin or sensitive bits. Before you chuck a handful of herbs into your bathtub and curse me for needing to clean the dang thing after, opt to add them in a gauze sachet so they don't make a mess of the tub. If you don't have a sachet, a sock works in a pinch—just be sure to tie it off!

If you're working with crystals in your bath, I strongly recommend NOT adding them directly into the water. Some crystals are not water-safe, meaning they can deteriorate or even rust when exposed to water for prolonged periods. Additionally, some crystals can leach toxins into the bathwater that you don't want to absorb into your skin, while others can scratch your bathtub. It's best to keep crystals on the edge of your tub or around your tub on the floor, but not directly exposed to water.

Finally, we need to talk about chemistry. Epsom salt is AWESOME for soothing the body and cleansing your energy, but when combined with certain soaps, it can create soap scum. If you hate cleaning your bathtub, maybe skip the Epsom salt when working with other soaps or opt for another type of salt.

While you soak, play some soothing music or read a book—anything to get you out of your head and into the vibe of your intention. A ritual bath is a great little treat after cleaning the bathroom or anytime you want to infuse your body and mind with a Magical intention!

Add the ingredients that follow to a sachet and toss it in your bath for a mess-free ritual! Don't have a sachet? No problem—grab a sock, fill it and tie it up, then toss it in. No bathtub? No problem! Turn any of the ritual baths into a shower ritual by hanging the sachet over the showerhead so the water streams through it. For the shower, a sock is a bit heavy, so you can opt for using the foot of pantyhose instead. Here are a few ritual baths to get you started, but there's also an entire list of recipes in the appendix of this book for you to explore (page 283).

Self-Love Ritual Bath

- Rose petals
- Lavender bubble bath
- Salt *for protection*
- Rose quartz

Creativity Ritual Bath

- Calendula petals
- Orange essential oil
- Lavender
- Epsom salt
- Citrine

Cleanse and Protect Ritual Bath

- Salt
- Lemon
- Cloves
- Black tourmaline

Abundance Ritual Bath

- Salt
- Cinnamon
- Bay leaves
- Calendula flowers
- Peppermint bubble bath

Getting your hair cut

Have you ever noticed that when you go through a major life transition, you feel pulled toward changing your hair? That's no accident! Your hair holds trauma, memories, and energy. So creating a ritual around cutting your hair with the intention of releasing stagnant energy and/or welcoming in fresh energy not only helps you move forward in your life but also reminds you to keep up with it. If it's been a while since your last haircut, you might feel stuck or stagnant. Depending on how often you need to get a trim, this can be a great full moon ritual or solstice/equinox ritual! As an added Magical bonus, you could journal your intention of what you are releasing before the cut and physically snip up the paper to aid in this release!

Shaving

Whether it's your face or your armpits, shaving can be annoying, so let's make it a little more Magical. First of all, whatever you use to shave has a Magical correspondence to it: shaving cream is great for growth and expansion (think of how it expands as you dispense it), while your razor has a Color Magic correspondence to it (refer to the Color Magic chart in Chapter 2, page 45). You can also add your own intentions to the shaving experience by drawing sigils on your shaving supplies.

Remember how hair holds memory, trauma, and energy from the time it grows? When you remove these hairs by shaving, consider it a deeeeep purge of old energy from your system.

Exfoliating

Every seven years your skin cells completely turn over, and since the skin is your body's largest organ, we often associate this with a transformation of the self. Consider exfoliation as an act of initiating that transformation. What do you want to release? What are you ready to let go of? Hold that in your awareness as you slough off the dead skin cells of your body. Bonus points if you choose an exfoliation product with a scent that matches your intention—try one of the following recipes for starters, or make your own and follow it with lotion as described next! Afterward, notice how much lighter you feel physically, energetically, and emotionally.

Coffee Scrub to Speed Up Spells

If you've been doing any kind of manifesting lately, this coffee scrub can speed up the process by adding a little extra OOMPH into your spells!

- ½ cup coffee grounds
- A dash of cinnamon
- ½ cup coconut oil

Self-Love Sugar Scrub

- ½ cup white sugar
- A dash of rose *(petals or oil)*
- ½ cup honey

Cleanse and Protect Salt Scrub

- ½ cup sea salt *or* Himalayan salt
- ½ cup oil *(coconut, almond, or jojoba are great options!)*
- 1 to 2 drops of mint oil *or a* dash of dried mint leaves

Applying lotion

You either love or hate this task. If you hate it, it's probably because it feels sticky and gross. If you love it, and since you're reading this book, you probably forget to do it regularly even though you know you want to. Try this to make lotion more Magical, enjoyable, and memorable!

For this, you'll need a lotion that doesn't give you the ick. Something quick-absorbing that doesn't feel sticky or slimy and is also either fragrance-free or with a scent you LOVE. We're going to turn this into a Magic spell for self-love, so take the time to find a product you truly enjoy!

To begin, draw a self-love sigil on the bottle—or you can just draw a heart! Place it on your counter and surround it with rose quartz crystals. Because rose quartz is one of the most popular stones for self-love, the crystal will infuse your lotion with the energy.

Now write down four things you like about yourself—these can be big or small, and don't be discouraged if it's hard to come up with them. Some examples are: *I am a good friend, I make really delicious pizza,* or *I love my button nose.* Don't skip this step!

As you rub lotion into one of your arms, repeat the first affirmation either out loud or in your head. Imagine rubbing that feeling of self-love into your skin, allowing it to absorb with the lotion. Repeat on the other arm and then each leg, picking a different affirmation for each limb.

Now, for the rest of your body, allow yourself to go off script—maybe something new comes to mind that you love about yourself, or maybe you simply want to express gratitude to your body. A simple *I love you* is always an option. Feel yourself enveloped in love and compassion.

Repeat daily, either with the same affirmations or with a new list every day. Notice how your relationship to yourself begins to deepen.

Taking medication

Some witches have mixed opinions about medication, but this witch doesn't. If you're prescribed medication, you should take it. Period. Don't listen to the spiritual "gurus" who say medication will stifle your intuition—it's bullshit. In fact, I have never felt more intuitive than when my Prozac dosage was corrected. When it comes to medication, you're likely using it to manage your brain, your health, or your pain, aka things that will be louder than your intuition when left unchecked. So see taking your meds as a practice of supporting your intuition. That said, maybe you forget to take them. Here are some Magical ways to fix that.

Crystals are a great tool to remember to take your meds. If you have one of those pill holders with a slot for each day, grab a handful of small crystals that help support the intention of your medication. Make a grid using the crystals to surround your medicine bottles, and each day you take your meds, move one of the small crystals into the slot that your pills were in. (Be sure not to swallow the crystals, though!) At the end of the week, you'll have an empty grid and a container full of crystals. Remake your grid, reset your intention, and refill your pill container. This is a great way to infuse your pills with the intention of your crystals AND give you a visual reminder to take your meds.

You can also add sigils into the mix here. If your medication helps with anxiety, perhaps you draw a relaxation sigil onto the bottle. If your medication helps you with an illness or disease, maybe you choose a healing sigil. If your medication is something you take every day, maybe you create a sigil for something you want to manifest and use your daily pill as an opportunity to focus your attention on that goal.

Finally, once you've finished your pill bottle, save it to use as a spell jar. You can add crystals, herbs, slips of paper with your intention written on them, anything you have on hand that will pull your focus to that intention. Add it to the bottle and keep it with you, or leave it on your altar. Anytime you want to reconnect with that intention, you can give it a shake!

Medication reminders for pets

If your pet needs regular medication, there's an opportunity here to impart some extra Magic into their routine. Draw a sigil for health and longevity onto the bottle of medication. If your pet needs a treat when taking their meds (who doesn't?), you can add a sigil to the treat bag as well. Finally, when dosing your pet, offer them words of affirmation. This could be as simple as "Good girl" or "You're so brave." Whatever feels right in the moment is probably what they need most.

Washing your mouth guard or dentures

Stagnant energy sitting in your mouth 24/7 is the last thing you want—so let's clear it while also washing your mouth guard or dentures! Using a bit of moon water and whatever cleanser you prefer, set the intention that anything blocking you from clear communication dissolve as you clean. Bonus—you can add a sigil to the cleanser package before you begin as a way to help you with public speaking or peaceful confrontation.

Once your mouth guard feels squeaky clean (physically AND energetically), set the intention that it support you throughout the day before placing it back into your mouth. Each time you become aware of it in your mouth, re-cement your intention. Notice if you communicate with yourself or others differently throughout the day!

Doing skincare

Infusing Magic into your skincare routine can be as simple or elaborate as you want. Maybe your skincare routine is a fifteen-step ritual that leaves you looking like a glazed donut or perhaps you simply want to stop falling asleep with mascara on. Choose any of the following options that feel inspiring to you, or try them all together to create a more detailed ritual.

To begin, create a sigil for the intention you want to use in your skincare routine. Think about what kind of intention you want to place on your skin. Self-love is always a good option when working with the skin, but you may also want to explore a sigil for protection, confidence, or courage. Create the sigil based on your product's uses: protective for SPF, releasing and purifying for cleanser, self-love for anti-aging toner, intuition and clear sight for eye creams, etc. You can use one sigil for each step of your skincare routine or make a different one for each! Once you've chosen your sigil, write it on the product container. As you apply each product, hold that intention in your awareness as if you were drawing the sigil on your face like armor.

For you crystal lovers, grab a crystal that suits your intention and place it near your skincare products. Clear quartz is great for amplifying intentions and rose quartz for self-love, and for my anxious friends you can't go wrong with smoky quartz. Allow the crystals to infuse into the products when you are not using them, then connect with that energy each time you apply the products.

Applying sunscreen

Sunscreen is a protection ritual at its finest! Think of how the SPF literally protects you from the sun's rays. Apply sunscreen with the intention that it also protect you from the energy you're encountering throughout the day from other people or places. Amp this up by creating a protection sigil—draw it on your sunscreen bottle AND draw it on your skin with the sunscreen before rubbing it in. As you rub the lotion on, imagine your energy field becoming stronger, more fortified, so any energy that doesn't serve you bounces off it throughout the day. I often imagine this like the shield that covers the ship in *Star Trek,* an invisible membrane separating my energy from everyone else.

Applying makeup

Use Color Magic here to your advantage! What intention do you want to set for your day? What energy do you want to call in? What do you have going on today that could use some extra support? Choose your blush, eye shadow, and lipstick colors to bring in that energy.

As you apply your makeup, sit with the energy that you're calling in. It's also a great time to pull in some affirmations that support that intention. For each step of your makeup routine, say a different affirmation. Consider using that selection of affirmations for a week or a month, and notice any difference in the way you feel!

Brushing your hair

This is a fantastic ritual for when you're feeling stuck mentally. When your hair is all tangled up, energy isn't able to flow through your mind as easily, so the thoughts build up. You can begin to untangle the mind by untangling your hair.

As you brush your hair, imagine untangling the tension and thoughts that have been looping through your mind. As your hair becomes tangle-free, feel the energy flowing more smoothly through your head and mind. Let your hair be a representation of how you're feeling mentally, and notice if you feel a shift after brushing through your strands!

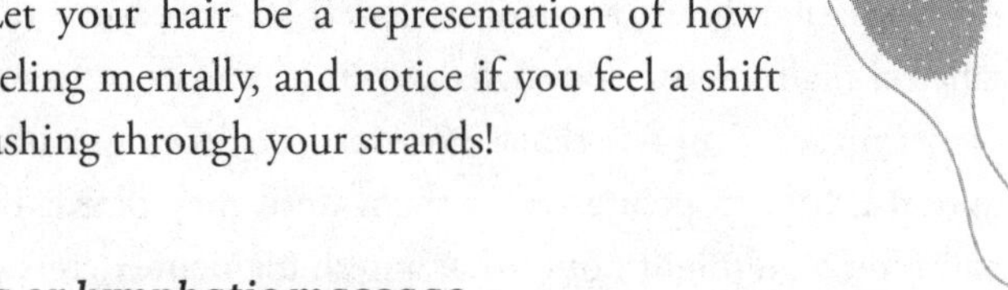

Gua sha or lymphatic massage

Your lymphatic system can get backed up much like your energy system can get blocked. Creating a gua sha, or lymphatic massage, ritual is a great option to regularly clear energy blockages in the body as well as to imbue your skincare routine with some self-love.

Enchant your massage tool by drawing a sigil on it, whether you use a dry brush or the crystal gua sha. Pick your tool with the intention of clearing stagnant energy and replacing that energy with compassion toward yourself. Apply an oil to your face before using your tool to allow it to glide over your skin. You can also opt for oils that align with your intention. Here are a few ideas to get started:

OIL	MAGICAL INTENTIONS
Jojoba	Love, emotional resilience
Coconut	Purification, protection, confidence
Grapeseed	Mental clarity, money, focus
Almond	Success, banishing, grounding, clarity, abundance, healing
Rose	Anti-anxiety, self-love, intuition, healing, protection, luck

As you massage your skin, feel or visualize the energy clearing in that area. Notice how your energy feels before and after the massage. Do you feel lighter? Does your brain feel less cluttered?

Nail care

Are you a nail-biter or a nail-peeler? If so, you know the importance of maintaining your nails and cuticles. As a constant cuticle-picker myself, I notice that whenever I neglect my nails, I create opportunities to pick away at them until they bleed. If you're a nail-biter, you might notice that a fresh manicure deters you from nibbling. While you're filing your nails or oiling your cuticles, repeat a few affirmations to yourself. This could be the same affirmation over and over or a different one for each finger. Allow the words to ground you in the present moment and remind you why taking care of your nails is important to you.

If you wear nail polish, you can add sigils and Color Magic to your nail care ritual. Draw sigils on the bottle of nail polish, or use clear nail polish to draw sigils on your nails to keep your intentions at your fingertips—literally.

Finally, what better way to add Color Magic into your day than with nail polish? Opt for a black polish for protection or a blue for calm. If you choose your nail polish based on what color calls out to you, ask yourself what that color may be providing you. How is it giving you the energy you need? Use this as an opportunity to meditate on the color while you paint each nail.

Nail trims for pets

As the owner of a dog who absolutely hates getting his nails trimmed, I've discovered a few ways to make his pedicure a little more Magical for both me and my pup. Whether you're going out to get their nails trimmed or doing it at home, you can begin to warm your pet up to the idea by touching their feet and offering them a reward. Treats, of course, make this Magical for your pet, but I've added an affirmation of gratitude each time I do it. Choose something specific you love about your pet. As you touch their feet, offer them this affection and give them a treat. Some examples I've used:

- I love that you snuggle under the covers in bed.
- I love that you look at me with your cute eyes.
- I love when you give a big sigh as you relax.
- I love when you wiggle your tail before eating dinner.
- I love your cute lil ears.

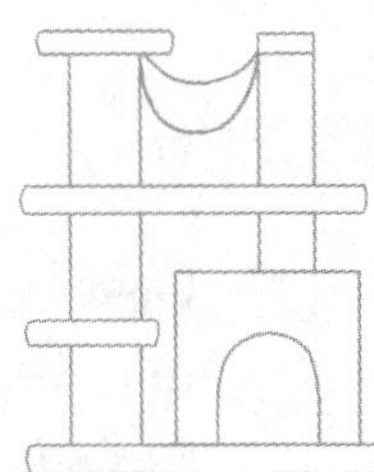

Now, when you go to clip your pet's nails, they should be more adjusted to the idea. Give them that same affection, naming ten things you love about them or are grateful for. This will help both you and your pet stay calm during the process.

Magical Upkeep

Cleaning the toilet

Your toilet is the prime place to add Magic into your bathroom. Believe it or not, when you use the toilet your body naturally clears energy from your field. If you've ever had a powerful energy-healing session and had to pee right after or felt like you had to pee when you entered a crystal shop, this is why!

You can use the toilet as a tool to keep your energy clear throughout the day—each time you relieve yourself, ask that any energy that doesn't belong to you be released into the bowl.

Now, because we're releasing energy into this thing, it's important we keep the toilet cleansed of any stagnant energy! Take your bathroom cleaner, stick it on your windowsill overnight—now you've got moon water in there to help cleanse the energy.

For cleaning the bowl, you can assign an intention based on the scent of your toilet bowl cleaner and draw a sigil into the bowl with the toilet brush. Preferably use a sigil that you want to flush down the drain—think a sigil to release anything holding you back from your intention, or a protection or cleansing sigil.

The underside of the toilet often collects dust, which we know means it's also collecting energy. Spend some extra time here with the intention of removing that stagnant energy and bringing the energetic frequency of your throne back to a neutral state.

Finally, take your bathroom spray and charge it up with some energy. To do so, you can use Reiki, a sigil, or speak your affirmations to it. Now every time you use the spray, you're spreading that intention throughout your bathroom!

Replacing the toilet paper roll

This is a great opportunity to infuse your space with an intention! Grab an essential oil that aligns with what you want to call into your space Magically. Add a few drops to the cardboard inner tube of your toilet paper roll and place it back on the holder. The scent will fill your space and inspire you to replace the roll next time!

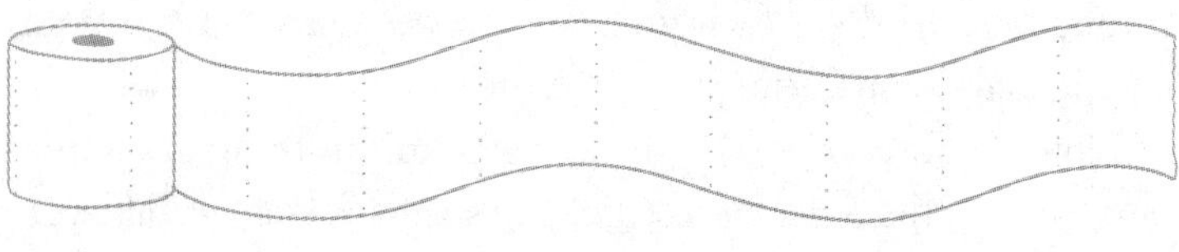

Scooping the litter box

We can use the litter box as a sort of sandbox to practice gratitude. As you scoop, call in the feeling of appreciation you have for your cat, saying an affirmation of gratitude with each turd you pick up. When adding new litter to the box, consider drawing a protection sigil on the container to keep your kitty safe and happy!

Cleaning the sink

If the bathroom is connected to abundance, then the sink allows that abundance to flow. When the sink is gunked up with toothpaste, hair, and other debris, your abundance might feel stagnant or stuck. Draw a sigil for abundance or the symbol for your currency on your bathroom cleaner and get to work clearing the obstacles to your prosperity by cleaning your sink. As you wipe, experiment with wiping in a counterclockwise motion to clear any obstacles blocking you from wealth, then wipe in a clockwise motion to invite abundance into your space.

Cleaning the tub and shower

Need some motivation to clean the tub and shower? Prepare a ritual bath for yourself in advance. Now, with the bathroom cleaner that you added your sigil to, spray down your shower walls and tub. Just as we cleaned the sink, wipe in counterclockwise motions to banish anything holding you back from enjoying this ritual bath and the intention you've set for it. Scrub clockwise to invite that intention into your tub and shower, exploring the following meditation for more Magic. Rinse and begin drawing your bath as a reward!

MEDITATION

Scrubbing the Shower

Begin by feeling your feet on the ground. Notice the connection between your big toe, pinkie toe, and heel. Keep part of your awareness on that connection throughout the meditation.

Now spray your cleaning spray, grab your gloves and sponge, and begin scrubbing. As you suds up the soap, smell the aromas of the soap. Notice how your body responds to the scent; where do you feel that response in your body? Can you still feel your feet on the floor?

As you scrub each part of the shower, the debris you're removing represents the energy you've collected throughout your day/week/life. Imagine that energy sloughing off your aura, releasing from your body and mind, and going down the drain. Perhaps you time this with your breath—scrub as you breathe in; release the energy from your space as you exhale. Keep your breath natural—there's no rush here!

Once again, feel your feet on the floor. Notice the pull of gravity softly tugging you down toward the earth. Invite this gravitational pull to gently draw anything you're ready to release and let go of out of your body and mind, into the earth. Here it can be transformed into new energy, new life, just as food scraps in a compost bin can turn into fertilizer.

Repeat this process until your shower is cleaned. Notice how you feel—has anything shifted physically, emotionally, energetically? Finally, rinse any lingering energy off your hands to complete the process.

Cleaning glass shower doors

When the glass of your shower door is fogged with soap scum, it can be hard to see clearly out of it. Think of this like a window into your manifestations and future goals. How clearly can you see them come to life in your experience? Visualize your goal as if you've already achieved it as you clean the scum off your shower doors. Let yourself marinate in the feeling and emotions of this manifestation as you clarify your intentions and clean the shower door until it sparkles!

Bathing pets

If your pet roams freely about your home, think of them like an energetic air purifier. Pets are especially sensitive to the energy of spaces; as they move through your home, they pick up energy that may be stagnating and they spread their own energy as they leave their fur around the place. When bathing your pet, see this as a way of clearing not only their energy but the energy of your home and yourself, too.

Consider grabbing a shampoo for your pet based on the Magical intentions of its ingredients, making sure to choose pet-safe ingredients! Perhaps you grab a relaxing scent for your anxious dog or an energizing scent for your lethargic cat—for pets with sensitive skin, a sigil on the bottle will work just as well!

As you work the soap into a lather, imagine it picking up all the energetic debris your pet has collected in their fur. As you rinse your pet's coat, wash that energy away. Dry your pet off while sending loving energy out through your heart and hands, allowing them to bask in your appreciation.

Taking out the bathroom trash

Use Color Magic to clear blocks and obstacles from your manifestations while you take out the bathroom trash! First, ask yourself, *What mental block is holding me back from this goal?* If you have a set of colored trash can liners, grab one that matches your intention. Or simply place a colored sticky note in the bottom of your trash can. Every time you throw something away, imagine tossing a bit of that mental block away with it. As you collect the trash at the end of the week, you banish that mental block for good.

Cleaning mirrors

Enchant your mirror for self-love with positive affirmations! Set a rose quartz next to your mirror to remind yourself that you are worthy of receiving your own compassion and kindness. Next, draw a self-love sigil (or a heart) on the glass cleaner bottle and spray your mirror. Clean in clockwise motions to draw the self-love into yourself while stating things you like about yourself mentally or out loud. Finally, lock in your self-love and protect yourself from negativity by drawing a protection sigil into the mirror with the rag.

Washing makeup brushes

If you wear cosmetics, cleaning your makeup brushes is the perfect way to add a bit of energetic protection into your routine. If you use a bar soap for cleaning them (unscented is best!), carve a sigil for protection into it with a toothpick or a quartz crystal point. If you use a liquid makeup brush cleanser, write the sigil on the bottle.

As you swirl your brush into the cleanser, imagine all the energy you've picked up throughout the week being drawn out of the brush. As you rinse the suds away, you're washing that stagnant or unwanted energy down the drain.

Now take a clean, dry cloth and swirl your brush into it gently to dry the bristles. Swirl in the shape of your protection sigil and place it with the bristles pointing down, so all the excess water and energy can drain out as it finishes drying.

Deep Magic

Cleaning the shower curtain liner

This is the ultimate full moon ritual for many reasons. The shower curtain liner is the perfect example of how energy builds up over time. Just as the soap scum, mildew, and water stains build up on your shower curtain, energy in your space builds up over time. By cleaning the shower curtain, you have a visual reminder that you are clearing your space. I love this task because it's easy (way easier than you're expecting) and makes a noticeable difference in my space! I used to have to throw out my shower curtain liner every few months because it got gross. Now that I wash it every full moon, I can keep the same liner for over a year, which is better for my space, my wallet, and our planet.

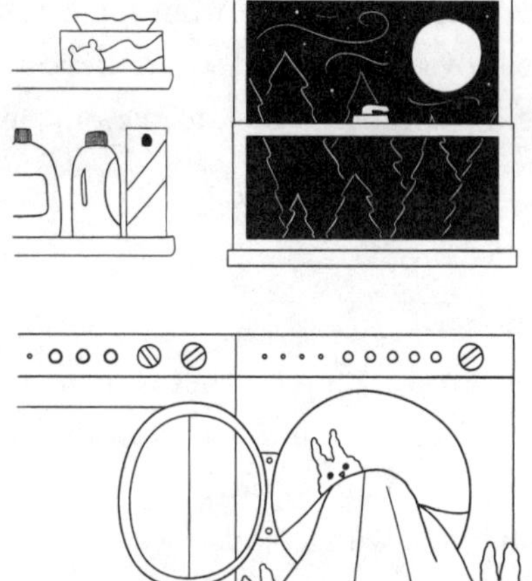

Grab your shower curtain off the hooks and toss

it right into your clothes washer with some towels. The towels act as an abrasive to rub the scum off the shower curtain. This works for plastic and fabric liners; just be sure you choose a water temperature appropriate for the curtain you are using. Now add in your detergent, a splash of moon water or Florida Water to help with the cleansing, and let the machine do all the work.

While it's washing, wipe down the shower curtain rod and the top of your showerhead or any other area in your bathroom that collects dust but doesn't get cleaned weekly.

Once clean, if it's a fabric liner, you can toss it in the dryer (check the heat settings for your liner!); if it's plastic, you can hang it in the shower to dry. Notice how much fresher your space feels by doing this super simple task!

Under sink and medicine cabinet clean-out

Since the bathroom is associated with wealth and prosperity, we want to ensure the sink has a good flow of energy to it. Check under the sink for any leaks; addressing these will help you fix any leaks in your flow of money. Now make sure that energy can flow under the sink to keep the wealth in your home flowing smoothly. Collect expired products or items you simply do not need and discard them. Corral the rest of your products under the sink into baskets or bins so the energy can flow around them. Finally, purge items from your medicine cabinet in the same way, ensuring that the energy can flow through all the spaces in your bathroom without being blocked by clutter.

If you have expired cosmetics or products you don't like to use anymore, repurpose them for spell jars! Chop up powdered makeup and separate by color to add a dash of Color Magic into your spells. Use creams and liquids to represent the spell's intention merging with your energy in the jar to increase its potency!

Cleaning the exhaust fan

Speaking of good energy flow, what better way to make sure energy is flowing than to clean and test your bathroom's exhaust fan? To test that it's working, grab a square of toilet paper and hold it up to the exhaust fan while it's on. A properly functioning exhaust fan should suck the paper up, holding it in place against the vent's grille. If you see this happen, that means the air (and energy) in your bathroom is properly venting to the outside—awesome! If not, it may be time to call for a repair.

Next, put some moon water on a rag and cleanse the dust from the outside of the fan grille. Now open up the grille and use a can of compressed air to blow the dust and debris off the fan blades.

As you shower, you are cleansing your energy, which is then sent into the air and sucked out via this fan. So all of that dust is stagnant energy, waiting to be cleared away. Doing this often will help your energy feel so much clearer—it's a good task to add to a new moon or full moon ritual!

Clearing out the linen closet

Instead of seeing clearing out the linen closet as a chore, see it as an opportunity to spread kindness. As you gather up old towels, blankets, and sheets, consider donating them to a local animal rescue. Sit with the feeling of giving back to these animals and the joy these objects will experience. For new or partially used toiletries, consider posting them in your local Buy Nothing group so someone else can use them. Sit with the feeling of offering kindness outwardly without the need for an immediate return, and feel your heart expand to invite kindness back to you! For the miscellaneous odds and ends, consider whether these items still hold a use for you: place them back into the closet with reverence if so, or if there's someone who can make better use of them, give them away with kindness.

Cleaning your toothbrush

It's recommended that you replace your toothbrush every three to four months, making this the perfect solstice/equinox ritual. What better way to welcome in the fresh seasonal energy than by tossing out the old energy collected on your toothbrush! After you replace the toothbrush, consider doing a deep clean of your teeth to clear out any stuck energy—this could be a trip to your dentist or spending a few extra minutes flossing and brushing as a seasonal shift ritual.

Cleaning hairbrushes

Grab your hairbrushes for a quick cleansing practice: Fill your sink with warm water and a bit of shampoo. Set the intention that any energy your brushes have collected be cleared away as you soak the brushes in the sink. Finally, give them a good rinse to release any energy they may have collected. Since your hair holds a ton of energy, you will likely feel a difference such as clarity of mind or clearheadedness the next time you brush your hair!

Chapter 7

Bedroom

Caring for your bedroom is critical for energetic maintenance and hygiene. The bedroom is a space of rest, rejuvenation, and pleasure. Therefore, it's important that the energy in this space reflect those qualities! Consider this when choosing furniture and decor for your bedroom—does that duvet cover help you embody these qualities? By tuning in to how the decor and colors in your space make you feel, not only will you become more in touch with yourself and your own energy, but you'll be able to make choices that help you align with your intentions in this space and beyond it so much more freely.

Energetic stagnation can impact your sleep as well. Have you ever had a night where you toss and turn without reason? Ever slept well but woke up feeling exhausted? When this happens night after night, without any rational reason behind it, there's a high likelihood that the energy in your bedroom is to blame.

Think of it like this: If your bedroom was filled with stinky trash, would you find it difficult to sleep? If there was a cacophony of noises in your bedroom, would you feel rested in the morning? Our body responds to cluttered energy like our conscious brain responds to an influx of smells or sounds—it's distracting. Remember your survival-based brain? When there's a ton of energy around, your brain is busy sorting through whether or not that clutter is dangerous. In contrast, the energy in a clear space is balanced and cleansed—your brain has less to fret about and can shut off for the night. So, if you struggle with sleep, prioritize the energy in your bedroom and notice how it shifts the way you feel at night!

Let's clear the stagnant energy and create a comforting space to rest by adding some Magic to the bedroom!

Daily Rituals

Going to bed on time

Have you ever heard of "revenge bedtime procrastination"? This is the practice of sacrificing a good night's sleep for activities like doomscrolling or otherwise putting off going to bed on time. This often comes up when we feel like we don't have control over our time during the day or when we don't make enough time for leisurely activities during the day. There's no shame in procrastinating your bedtime—we ALL do it from time to time, and sometimes a long scroll down the Instagram feels fun and entertaining. But if you find it gets in the way of your sleep or feels icky in your body, you may want to substitute the scrolling for a bit of Magic instead!

Before bed is the perfect time to cleanse your energy from the day and set an intention for the night ahead. It's a powerful time to manifest. Incorporating even two minutes of Magic into your bedtime routine can break that habit of bedtime procrastination and help you sleep better at night, leading to a more rested morning! Choose one of these ideas to add to your routine tonight and see how your sleep improves:

Two-minute evening routine ideas

- Before falling asleep, set an intention to meet your spirit guides.
- Cleanse your bedroom with incense, sound, or a lavender spray.
- Have a cup of tea that aligns with the intention of good sleep. 
- Draw a sigil on your skin with a relaxing essential oil roller.
- Write down three things from your day that brought you joy.
- Use Color Magic to choose your pajamas for the evening.
- Keep crystals for sleep (like amethyst, celestite, or black tourmaline) under your pillow or next to your bed.
- Pull a tarot or oracle card with the intention of reflecting on your day.

- While in bed, ask your body how it wants to move before bed and allow yourself to roll around or stretch in bed for a few breaths.

- Do a few minutes of Reiki or meditation before bed.

- Create a nightstand altar (instructions below) and spend some time there before bed.

- Place a sleep bowl on your nightstand (instructions on page 185).

- Read a Magical book (like this one!) before bed and plan to incorporate one spell into your day tomorrow. Write it down in your calendar so you don't forget!

Nightstand altar

Intention starts with your environment. Use your nightstand to prompt you to begin your new nighttime routine, but also to create a sacred and peaceful space for the best chance of sleeping well!

A nightstand altar is simple to create—it's an intentional space to commit to rest, peace, and sleep.

Some things you can place on your altar:

- Crystals for sleep: amethyst, celestite, and black tourmaline are my faves, but you can find more options in the Crystal Appendix of this book (page 297)!

- Herbs for sleep: chamomile, lavender, and mugwort are classic sleep herbs.

- A sleep bowl or written intention—check out the recipe on page 185!

- Gratitude journal.

- Tarot or oracle cards.

- Glass of water for protection—if you're someone who accumulates cups of water on your nightstand, set the intention that the water collect any energy you're clearing from your field while you sleep. Water a plant with it in the morning to transmute the energy and clear your space!

What you can do with your nightstand altar:

- Charge your hand cream, cuticle oil, or lip mask with intention.

- Connect with gratitude before bed.

- Set an intention to influence your dreams and sleep.
- Convince yourself to clear off the seventy-two cups of water you've left on your nightstand.

Falling asleep

Once the energy of your bed is clear, you may find that falling asleep and staying asleep feel much easier. But just in case, the powerful meditation on page 186 will discharge any pent-up energy in your body from the day and help you drift off into a state of rest!

Sleep Bowl Recipe

Studies have shown that reading an intention before bed or placing something that symbolizes your intention next to your bed can influence your dreams. This intention could help you sleep, meet your spirit guides, or answer a question if you're at a crossroads. Creating a sleep bowl is a great way not only to set that intention, but to be reminded of it each time you look at your nightstand.

INGREDIENTS:

- *Something to calm the mind:* **mint**, **fennel**, **lime**, *and/or* **fluorite**
- *Something to calm the body:* **lavender**, **chamomile**, **basil**, *and/or* **amethyst**
- *Your written intention:* **piece of paper**, **sigil**, or **bay leaf**
- *Something to help you fall asleep:* **rosemary**, **lavender**, *and/or* **celestite**
- *Something to protect your dreams:* **mugwort**, **salt**, *and/or* **black tourmaline**

Write your intention and place it in your bowl. Cover with a sprinkle of herbs and crystals. Before bed, read your intention to yourself, then place it back in your sleep bowl. Keep the sleep bowl on your nightstand altar. When you wake up, write down your dreams in a dream journal.

If you have cats, feel free to put a lid on the bowl or keep it in an organza bag. After all, your intention is more important than the vessel you choose!

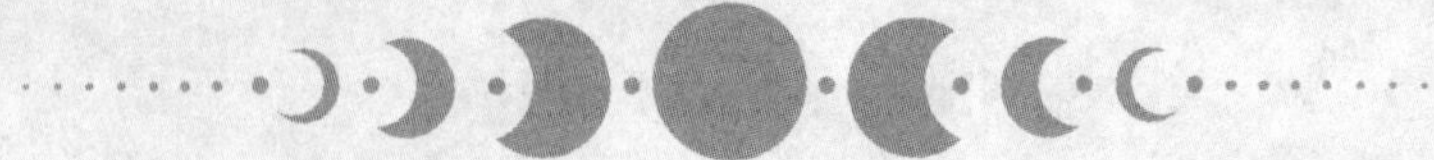

MEDITATION

Progressive Muscle Relaxation for Sleep

Lie down in your bed in whatever position you prefer to sleep in and take a couple of deep breaths.

As you breathe, let your shoulders release, let your jaw soften, feel the support underneath your body.

Without stressing your muscles out, using only about half your strength, squeeze the muscles in your face. Purse the lips, scrunch the nose, squeeze the eyes, almost like you just ate a lemon. You're trying to squeeze the smallest face you can make.

Feel that tension start to build. Take a breath in and feel it.

And with your exhale, release it fully and all at once. Let the face relax, the eyebrows, the eyes, the cheeks, the mouth, the tongue.

Now bring your awareness to your shoulders and gently squeeze the shoulders up toward your ears. Feel the muscles in your neck and upper back get tight.

Feel the energy start to build in this space. Take a breath in to feel it.

With your exhale, let it go. Let the shoulders drop. Maybe you swallow a few times to loosen up the throat.

Now begin to tense the muscles down the left arm, squeezing the bicep, the forearm. You can make a gentle fist with the fingers or spread the fingers wide. You might even feel a gentle shake in the left arm and hand.

Feel that tension build. Take a breath in.

Now release with your exhale. Feel the arm get heavy from the shoulder all the way down to the fingertips.

And notice the difference between the left and right side here. Does one side feel more awake? Does one side feel more soft? Does one side feel more heavy?

And now squeeze the muscles in the right arm in the same way. Bicep, lower arm, hand in a fist, or spread the fingers wide. Feel all the muscles in your right arm wake up.

Take a breath in to feel it, and a breath out to let it go.

Feel that softness from the shoulders all the way down to the fingertips. And feel that left and right side again. Notice if you feel more similarities now.

Now, keeping your breath flowing freely, squeeze the muscles in your chest, your back, and your abdomen. Feel that bracing through the torso.

Take a breath in, and with your exhale, soften through the whole center of your body. Let the abdomen relax, the chest soften. Feel that tension release from the whole upper body.

Now tense the muscles in the left leg. Squeeze the glutes, the thigh; curl the toes back toward your shin, spread them wide; feel the whole left leg. Wake up all the muscles activating here, keeping the rest of the body soft.

Take a breath in and feel it. And with your exhale, let it go. Feel the support underneath your hip, your leg, your foot.

Then do the same thing on the right side now, from the glute to the leg, all the way down; curl the toes back toward the shin, spread them wide; feel the whole right leg waking up.

Take a breath in, and let it go. Feel that support beneath your hip, your leg, your foot.

And now just notice the whole body, from head to toe, feeling any relaxation in the whole body.

Bring your awareness to your feet, wherever they make connection with the bed. Feel the support underneath you.

Take a deep breath in and let a full breath out.

If there's anywhere else in your body that feels tense, gently squeeze and release each part on its own.

Keep breathing deeply until you drift off to sleep.

Waking up early

Okay, tough love time, if waking up early is a struggle for you—I need you to prioritize your nighttime routine before your morning routine. When you're awake, it's easy to say, "Oh yeah, I'll wake up and do XYZ, which will get me out of bed." But if you have a rough night's sleep or are constantly exhausted, you need to address this FIRST (as covered in the first part of this chapter). But assuming your night routine is already Magical, here are a few ways to make waking up early more Magical. Add ONE of these ideas to your day tomorrow and see how it feels. Switch and swap as often as you want, but remember LESS IS MORE—so don't try to do EVERYTHING all at once!

Two-minute morning routine ideas

- Pull one tarot or oracle card. Take a photo of it and make it your phone's lock screen for the day, reflecting on the message throughout the day.

- Lay out your crystals and hover your hand over them. Choose the one that sings to you and carry it with you during the day.

- Take three deep breaths and scan your awareness down your body. Become curious about any parts of you that feel tense or relaxed.

- Before you leave the bed, ask your body how it wants to move today and allow yourself to roll around or stretch in bed for a few breaths.

- Play singing bowls or solfeggio tones while you get ready for the day.
- Using a spoon, stir the shape of a sigil into your coffee or tea based on how you're feeling in the morning and what kind of energy will most support your day.
- When you smell fresh coffee, name three things you are grateful for.
- Keep a spray bottle of moon water (for cleansing) or rosewater (for self-love) next to your alarm—when it chimes, spritz your face to wake yourself up!
- Change your alarm tone to a meditation or audio yoga practice.

Getting dressed

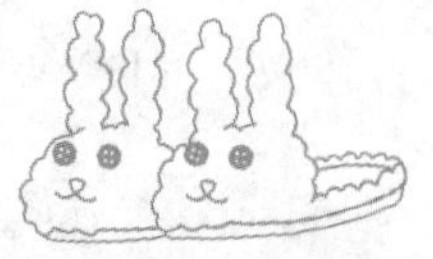

First, decide what energy you want to embody today: Is it a day where you need confidence? Feeling a little frazzled and want some calm? Think about the version of yourself that already embodies that energy. What kind of clothing do they wear? Are they dressed to the nines or chilling in sweats? Now, based on this energy, choose items of clothing that this version of you would wear. Bonus—you can choose pieces based on Color Magic to amplify this energy.

If your wardrobe isn't as colorful as you'd like, you can always embody Color Magic in your accessories: socks, scrunchies, nail polish, and colorful underwear are all subtle ways to carry Color Magic with you throughout the day.

Intimacy Magic

Sexual pleasure can be a pathway to deep rest and is deeply healing to your body when enjoyed consensually! Whether you're receiving pleasure from yourself, a toy, or a partner, you can add Magic to spice up this experience.

Here's a ritual to get in the mood: Add a drop of ylang-ylang oil to the insides of your ankles, drink or diffuse some damiana tea, and crack open your favorite fairy smut book to activate the Magic of your sacral chakra and prime your energy field for pleasure.

Remember that nightstand altar you made on page 182? Add some sensual elements to it, like your favorite vibrator or lubricant. Infuse these objects with the energy of pleasure by letting them rest in a space of pride rather than hiding them away! How you do anything is how you do everything, remember? So, when you shamelessly display these tools of pleasure, you're reaffirming that you deserve to feel pleasure!

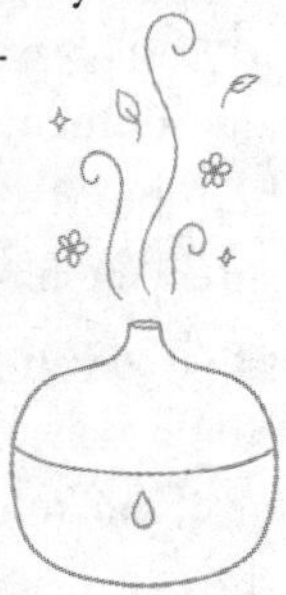

Finally, once you are fully satisfied, call into your awareness something you wish to manifest. Let your attention infuse this goal with the energy of pleasure and satisfaction so it can take root and grow into your life much faster!

Magical Upkeep

The bed

When you sleep, your energy field becomes more porous, naturally releasing unwanted energy you've picked up during your day.

The question then becomes: Where does that energy go? If you're not cleansing the energy of your mattress regularly, you're swimming in it!

Maybe you notice you haven't been sleeping as well as usual or you're waking up feeling groggy or heavy—these are all signs it's time to cleanse.

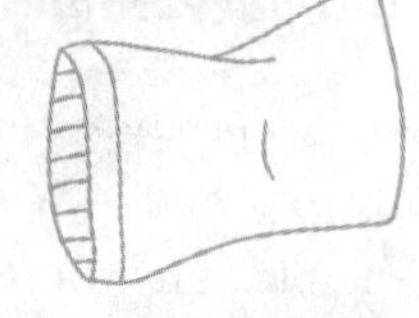

Luckily, we can clean the sheets and cleanse the mattress at the same time. Do this weekly and notice if you sleep better!

Cleaning the sheets

First, strip everything off the bed and wash your sheets with a little bit of moon water to assist in the cleansing process.

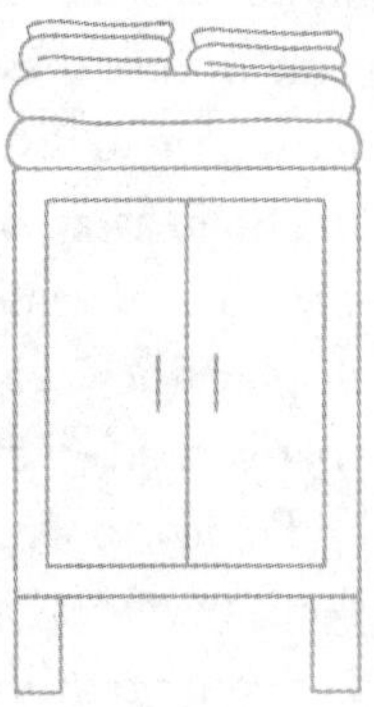

Now, to clear the energy of your mattress, you will need either smoke or sound—choose what makes the most sense for you and your environment. For smoke cleansing, wave your herb bundle or incense stick over the bed—be sure you have a fire-safe dish underneath to catch any rogue embers! For sound cleansing, ring a bell or singing bowl around your bed; or, if you're using music, place the speaker on the mattress for one song, then under the mattress for another.

Washing the duvet and pillows

After clearing the energy of your mattress, re-dress the bed with clean sheets and spritz with moon water or a lavender sleep spray for protection. If you have a duvet or pillow that you wash periodically, this could be a good opportunity to do a deep clean during the solstice or equinox.

Deep Magic

Cleaning under the bed

We also want to clear the energy underneath the bed; during the solstices or equinoxes would be a good time to sort out any clutter that may be hiding under there. The less you have under the bed, the less the energy will collect there, and the better you will sleep! While you're under there, sweep or vacuum any dust bunnies—these are energy magnets!

Cleaning pet bedding

Just as we shed unwanted energy while sleeping, so do our pets. Cleaning their bedding regularly is important to keep them feeling settled and sleeping well. Take caution to avoid using any cleanser that may harm your pet, so skip the smoke cleanse and anything with fragrances. Instead, opt for tossing anything washable in the laundry with a splash of moon water. For items that cannot be laundered, use sound to cleanse. Better yet, get your pet to make their happy noise to cleanse their bed! Give your cat extra love until they purr, using the vibration to clear energy from the space. Get your dog in a playful mood until they're panting with a big goofy grin on their face to clear away that stagnant energy!

Dusting blinds

Your blinds and curtains are the energetic force field protecting your bedroom. Glass windows can be used to see through, but they can also distort. Thus, the energy that passes through can be either cleared or manipulated by stagnant energy. By dusting your blinds, you're reinforcing that clarity, which ensures the energy of your space stays protected and clear.

To amp this up, use a bit of moon water to dust the windowsills and blinds. Wash curtains with a splash of moon water as well. When the sun is up, open the blinds so the sun can cleanse the energy of your bedroom with its powerful rays. Finally, keep a spray bottle of moon water or leave your favorite linen spray on the sill overnight and spritz your blinds or curtains anytime the energy could use a refresh.

*Organizing the bedroom closet**

As you move into the closet, use this opportunity to infuse energy into all the nooks and crannies of your bedroom. Sort your clothes based on how they make you feel and/or using Color Magic. What items make you feel confident? What items make you feel peaceful? What items make you a better communicator? Every season, as you set your intentions with the equinox or solstice, move the clothing items that align with this intention to the front of your closet. You might find that you no longer gravitate toward certain garments, which may indicate that they no longer fit your intentions. Therefore, you can release them from your space.

Grab your favorite clothing hanger (it's worth the splurge to buy a fancy wooden one for this!) and decorate it with intention. Turn it into a visual spell by adding colorful affirmations, adhering crystals, perhaps spritzing it with herb-infused moon water. Each evening, pick out your

I AM PROTECTED

* For more Magical advice, check out decluttering clothes in Chapter 4 on laundry (page 110).

outfit for the next day and hang it on the spelled hanger. As the clothing hangs from the spelled hanger, it infuses with your intention overnight. Bonus—it makes your morning routine just a little bit easier!

Decluttering sentimental items

Because our stuff holds memories, emotions, and energy, it's natural to feel attached to certain items—especially sentimental items that represent our youth or a previous version of ourselves. Often this attachment hides below the surface until we are faced with the idea of decluttering these items. Now, I'm a sentimental girlie at heart, so I'm all for keeping the token from the arcade your partner took you to on a first date. But when it comes to these sentimental items, less is often more. We can release the small attachments to a bunch of stuff and instead choose a selection of items with intentionality. This smaller collection therefore holds all those attachments and can represent a much deeper connection. Here are some ideas to get you started purging unwanted items that may hold sentimental value:

- **Hold a funeral for your past self:** If there is a version of you that you have outgrown (your emo phase in high school, your competitive swimming era, etc.), collect the items representing that and host a funeral for that version of yourself. Write a eulogy, express gratitude to yourself at that time, and decide how you'd like to memorialize that time in your life without stuff. Perhaps it's a photo in your scrapbook or saved to the favorites folder on your phone, or you could even get a tattoo to represent this version of yourself. Once you've memorialized this time, you don't need the stuff anymore—let it go.

- **Cleanse attachments:** Letting go of sentimental items can be particularly difficult when the attachments are still active. So, breaking that connection is the first step in deciding if this is really something you'd like to keep holding on to. Grab the first item you're considering releasing—perhaps it's one trinket or a whole box of memories. Hold it in your hands. As you inhale, feel the support of the universe enter your body. As you exhale, release the attachment to this stuff. Close your eyes and repeat this for a few breaths. When you reopen your eyes, imagine these items were on a shelf at your local thrift store. Would you pick them up? Would you bring them home? Where would you keep them?

- **Honor sentimental energy:** One way to keep sentimental clutter at bay is by treating your sentimental items with reverence. For example, I don't have many trinkets or items left behind by my grandmother, but I do have a pair of her earrings. I keep them on my altar in a shrine devoted to her, and thus they aren't clutter but powerful tools that represent her love and support. As you parse through sentimental objects, create an intention to treasure each item. Where will you place it in your home so you can enjoy the memories it evokes? How will you honor the memories attached to this item? This can help you get clear on which items really matter to you and which ones are just collecting dust.

Chapter 8

Office

Energy and productivity go hand in hand, so your office often represents your mental state. Notice your office right now: Does it feel spacious or cramped? Calm or chaotic? Cluttered or organized? Now notice your mind: Do your thoughts feel spacious or cramped? Calm or chaotic? Cluttered or organized? You probably have already noticed that when you have a really busy week at work, your office becomes more disheveled than the weeks when you have more space in your schedule. If you are chronically busy, making intentional efforts to keep your office space organized can actually help your brain feel more settled.

We know that our environment affects productivity. Painting your office certain colors can elicit different emotional states. Temperature can affect our focus, as can decor and the ergonomics of our desk setups. All these factors play into how the energy moves through your office space as well. When setting up your desk space, ask yourself: *What mental state do I want to be in when I sit down to work? What colors or decor bring me closer to that state? What do I need to remove from this space to feel this way?*

Your office is your sanctuary when at work. Whether you work from home, in a shared space, or at a private office, creating an intentional energetic space will allow you to work more productively and burn out less frequently.

Daily Rituals

Managing your to-do list and schedule

So you have a to-do list that's longer than a CVS receipt? Wondering how you will possibly tackle it all and simultaneously feeling bad about not doing enough? Cool, let's fix that.

Grab your colored pens for this—we're using Color Magic! Use a red pen to write the items that require more of your energy, purple ink for the things that require your focused attention, and blue ink for the tasks that require your communication skills.

Now that you've written your color-coded to-do list, write in black ink a few self-care tasks. This could be taking three deep breaths, eating lunch, or doing another Mundane Magic task. Spread these out throughout your list—don't bump them to the bottom! These are opportunities to reset your energy, especially as you switch from red to purple to blue tasks.

Now grab your calendar and block off time in your day to do these things. Use Color Magic here as well! Finally, set up alerts on your calendar or phone to remind you when to switch tasks—use affirmations for these. For instance, before you begin a block of red tasks, set the alert to "I am energized," or for purple tasks, "My mind is clear and focused." Maybe blue tasks have an alert that says, "May I speak with kindness and efficiency."

Making phone calls

Consider using your office phone as a mindfulness cue. Mindfulness cues are powerful ways to create an association in the brain—just as Pavlov trained dogs to salivate when they heard a bell, you can condition your brain to respond more mindfully to your office phone ringing! This is something I implemented when I was a support line advocate as a way to help regulate my nervous system when I got a crisis call. I still use it to this day.

Next time your phone rings, instead of picking it up on the first ring, take a deep breath. Don't worry—the person on the other end won't just hang up if you take three seconds to breathe first! After your exhale, smile and pick up the phone. Notice how this impacts the call? Prompting your cue is important at the beginning, so place a sticky note on your phone to remind yourself. After a while, it will become second nature. You can do this before making an outbound call as well!

Using emojis as sigils

Sigils are symbols, so in theory you can use ANY symbol as a sigil. Look at your most used emojis—what emotion do they evoke for you? Now choose an emoji for your intention and assign that energy to it just as you would a sigil.

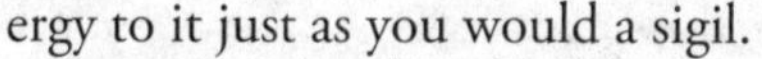

For instance, maybe you choose the sparkle emoji as a protection sigil. You can now use this in your social media profiles, or turn the transparency to 100 percent if you don't want it to be visible and place it in profile pictures or social media posts.

Remember: it doesn't need to be physically visible for the sigil to work—you could choose an emoji for abundance and invisibly add it to the background of your résumé. Perhaps you place an emoji for peace in the contact name for a person who really riles you up.

Answering emails and inbox management

Have you ever left an email unread so you'll "get to it later" but by the time later comes you have seventy-three other unread emails and now you're so overwhelmed you don't know where to start? Me too. Let's fix that.

Grab a tea light candle, then top it with mint for focus and rose for compassion. (Reminder that you can substitute these herbs for crystals or other ingredients you have on hand using the Ingredients Appendix, page 291, in the back of the book!) Light the candle with the intention of solely focusing on your inbox while the candle is lit.

As you go through each email, do not respond to them. Simply purge the ones that you know do not need a response. Clear that stagnant energy out of your inbox so you can get clarity on what needs to be done.

Next, tackle the "easy" emails. These require limited responses—think confirming a meeting, sending an attachment, a quick reply to a colleague, etc.

Unsubscribe from any email you don't even bother reading, which will clear the energy for your future inbox at the same time!

Now that you have some momentum, the energy should feel less heavy and dense. You can tackle those emails that require a more thorough response.

As the candle burns out or your timer goes off, offer a moment of gratitude and set the intention that those emails get sent to their destination with the energy of loving-kindness attached. Blow out the candle. You did it!

Magical Upkeep

Cleansing the energy in your office

As you look around your workspace, consider how you can create an environment to inspire creativity, productivity, and focus. If you work in a shared space, maybe this is simply a crystal that symbolizes those things for you that you can keep in the space or in your pocket while working. If you have a whole office to yourself, consider setting up an office altar with items to

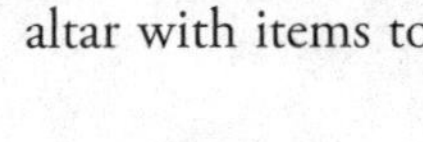

inspire your focus and support your goals at work. If you have a job that you hate but need to keep paying the bills, consider setting up a protection ritual and a money bowl to attract prosperity.

Before we even dive in to setting the energetic scene in your space, you'll want to cleanse the energy. Depending on your work, you'll need to do this regularly. If you work from home or in a tranquil environment, this may not need to be done every day, but if you work with the public or in a high-stress environment, you may consider making this a part of your daily routine.

Explore the following meditation and notice how it shifts the energy in your space today.

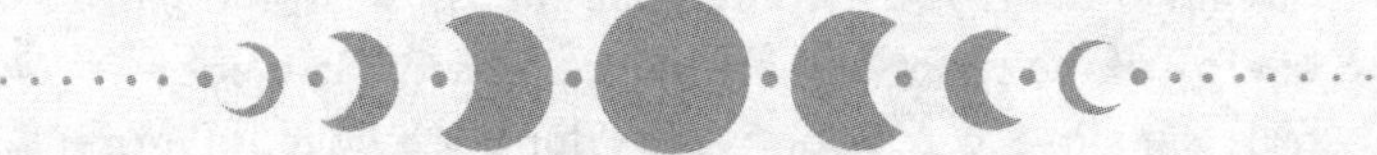

MEDITATION

Energy-Cleansing for Spaces

Go ahead and get comfortable. You don't have to be anywhere special in your space for this. But if you have a choice, somewhere in the middle might be helpful.

Take a couple of deep breaths. Let yourself settle in. Feel the parts of your body that make contact with the support beneath you. Your hips, your legs, your feet. See if you can settle into that support a little bit more.

Tune in to the space around you. Perhaps your eyes are closed or your gaze is fixed on one spot. With curiosity, feel the space around you. Are there parts that feel light and airy? Are there spaces that feel dense or heavy?

Are there spaces that feel open versus spaces that feel cluttered? Just tune in to it.

There's no right or wrong here. Let yourself become aware with your senses to the space around you. What does it feel like?

Then bring your awareness to your space, the space directly around you—where your energy ends and the energy of the room begins. Notice where those edges are. Is it close to your body? Is it further away? Is there a shape to it? A thickness?

This is all just play, just curiosity.

Now bring your awareness to your breath. And just notice that natural ebb and flow. The inhale turns into the exhale.

Feel the breath move into the body, down into the abdomen. Feel it change to become an exhale. Release it out of the body into the space around you.

And as you breathe in, imagine each breath is like a light, a great bright light moving into the body.

With each inhale that light is growing brighter and brighter, expanding through the chest. Fill the arms and legs, the whole body with this great bright light.

And each time you breathe in you draw in more light, becoming brighter and brighter.

The light becomes so bright that it expands beyond the edges of your body into the space around you, filling your whole energy field with light.

Each inhale fills you up with light, growing bigger and bigger. Let it expand to fill the space you're in. See it move to the parts that felt dense or heavy or stagnant before. The areas of clutter. Allow it to bring an element of airiness, of lightness to the space.

Feel that light expand to every nook and cranny from the floor to the ceiling to the walls. And as this light expands, let your awareness expand with it and feel the space around you. Has anything shifted?

If there's any part of the space that's still calling your attention, that still feels a little dense, focus the light there. As if you were shining a flashlight into any dense, sticky, or heavy energy that might be in the space still.

Take a deep breath in. Clear it out with your exhale.

Feel the light come back to your energy field. Back to your body. And tune in. Notice if you or the space feel different at all.

Take one more deep breath in. Clear the rest out with your exhale.

Cleaning your desk

Energetically, the state of your desk will reflect the state of your mind and vice versa. If your brain feels really cluttered, clearing off your desk can help release the chaos from your mind. Take a moment to check in on your mind—are you feeling scattered? Overwhelmed? Flustered? Now begin to remove clutter from your desk with the intention of also removing that clutter from your mind. As you sit back down to your tidy desk, notice how much more clarity you have to finish your work for the day!

Now that the clutter is off your desk and probably in a giant pile on your floor (just me? okay, cool), you'll want to declutter it from your space entirely. Whether it's a closet of doom or a box of bits and bobs, be honest with yourself about what is needed and what you can let go of. (You can find more tips for decluttering the living room in Chapter 3, page 69.) This will allow you to maintain a clear and focused mind throughout the workweek by releasing anything that's unnecessary from your space and mental energy. Consider making a note in your calendar to declutter each full moon.

Opening mail

You have a pile of envelopes—you assume they are bills or junk mail so you avoid opening them. This is often a reflection of the negativity bias in your brain. Your brain, for the purposes of survival, assumes the worst in a situation and prioritizes remembering negative information. For example, if you received twelve "Great job!" emails from your boss and one "You could have done this differently" email, your brain would zoom in on that one negative email and it would hold more weight for you mentally than the twelve positive emails. The good news is, with awareness we can shift focus to the positive—how you do anything is how you do everything, so opening the mail is a great opportunity to practice this!

Instead of assuming the letter you're about to open is junk or a bill, what if you imagined every piece of mail was a fun surprise? It could be a note from an old friend, a surprise check, or a letter from Taylor Swift inviting you backstage at her next show! Open each item with this excitement, but the trick is—don't let the negativity bias weigh you down if what you open isn't a fun surprise. Instead, practice curiosity. It could be a bill, but it could also be a note from Taylor . . . The only way to find out is to rip it open and see!

Going to the post office

Whether you need to buy stamps, pick up your mail, or drop off a package, the post office can be a chore we put at the bottom of the list again and again. This Magical ritual is going to motivate you to hit the PO but will also bring joy to not just you, but someone else as well.

Decide how often you need to go to the post office—whether it's quarterly, monthly, weekly, or more. Make a list of people in your life that you are grateful for, collect their addresses, and pick up a pack of postcards. Each time you visit the post office, write a note of appreciation for someone on your list and pop it in the mail. This simple act of kindness can infuse your entire day with gratitude, make your loved one smile, and transform your relationship to the post office into somewhere you can't WAIT to visit!

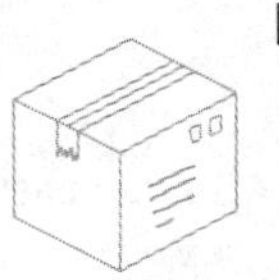

Shredding old paperwork

Old paperwork represents a past version of you, your career, your finances, your business, whatever the case may be. Take your favorite colored marker and write down your fears, negative self-talk, or anything else you want to release. As you shred each page, release the parts of your past that hold you back from becoming the best version of yourself now and in the future.

Finding motivation to work or study

The Magic of this task is in coming home to your why. Ask yourself: Why are you working or studying? What is the end goal of learning this information? Of doing this work task? Is it something you are passionate about or bringing you closer to a career that lights you up? Is it to put food on the table or to ignite your desire to help others? Once you've deeply reflected on your why, write that on a candle. Alternatively, you could create a sigil for your why and draw that in the wax. Before you begin studying or working, sit with your why as you light the candle. Set the intention that, while this candle burns, you will work with your why as a guiding light. When finished, blow out the candle and thank it for supporting you in this task.

Dealing with difficult coworkers or clients

People can be a real drain on your energy, no matter how sensitive you are to it. If you have an especially difficult coworker, consider a protection ritual such as carrying protective crystals, keeping salt in your desk drawer, or drawing protective sigils on your office door with your finger at the start of your day.

If you have a particularly difficult client, consider a disconnecting ritual after they leave your space. For instance, it could involve washing your hands. As you wash your hands, imagine their energy releasing from your body and energy field, sending it down the drain and back to the source.

If everyone around you is sucking you dry, consider the following meditation to turn your piss-poor mood back around.

MEDITATION

Reverse a Bad Mood

Find a comfortable place to sit. Chances are, if you're in a bad mood, you're probably in a weird, crumpled-up position on the couch or at your desk with your spine shaped like a shrimp. So, take a more intentional posture for this time.

You don't have to be in a perfect position, but make it an intentional position. Take a deep breath in, open your mouth, and sigh it out. Sigh it like you mean it.

Breathe in.

Make a noise as you exhale.

One more time.

Bring your awareness to the crown of your head and imagine your bad mood is like the sediment in a watering hose. With each breath, start to clear that sediment out.

As you inhale, breathe in through the crown of the head, feeling the breath move all the way down to the abdomen.

As you exhale, send the breath down the legs, out the soles of the feet.

Breathe in from the crown to the abdomen, breathe out from the abdomen to the soles of the feet.

Like you're pushing that bad mood out of your body, into the earth. The earth can take it. The earth can transmute it like compost turns back into nutrients in the soil. Let the earth carry that bad mood away; you don't need to hold it.

Now think of this practice as kind of like a turkey baster: You're sucking in good, new, fresh energy from the crown of the head to the abdomen. And then you're squeezing that turkey baster out, pressing all that sediment out through the legs, out the soles of the feet.

So if that visual helps you, or if it just makes you chuckle a little, you're welcome. But keep going, a couple more breaths here.

With your next inhale, take an even deeper breath in. The deepest breath you've taken today. Now sigh it out with a sound.

Wiggle your legs, shake your arms, shake your shoulders, shake your head—really shake that bad mood out.

As you return to stillness, bring into your awareness something that you want to do, something that will make you feel energized, motivated. Not what you *have* to do or *should* do. What do you *want* to do?

Become aware of the first step of that thing. If your desire is to go for a walk, maybe the first step is putting your socks on. If it's eating a candy bar, maybe it's opening up your pantry. If it's taking a nap, maybe it's grabbing a blanket. What is the first, easiest step to do that thing?

Can you imagine what it would feel like to take that first step? Can you see yourself doing it, or feel yourself doing it?

Now stand up, open your eyes, and go do the dang thing.

Overcoming creative blocks

The number one ingredient for creativity is play! Play, play, play. Something we don't do enough of, especially when we're trying to be creative for whatever reason. The following meditation is designed to help activate that playfulness, get you out of your head, and allow your creativity to shine through.

You can set a timer to do this, or go until you fill the page. Don't put pressure on yourself for how long it needs to be.

Maybe you even notice just a bit of relaxation in the body as you do this, too. If you're taking it too seriously, if you're all stressed out, maybe check yourself. It's supposed to be fun and a little silly.

MEDITATION

Doodling to Activate Creativity

For this practice, you'll need something to write with and something to write on. It could be lined paper, a journal, or even a napkin.

Step 1. Uncap your pen.

Step 2. Get out of your head. If you're not really a doodler, you might find it challenging at first, but I promise it gets easier.

Ready? Now place your pen to the paper and take a couple of deep breaths.

Get out of your head and just let the pen move. Don't think about what you are making, where this is going, what it looks like. Just let yourself draw.

It could make sense; it could make no sense. Just let yourself doodle. Could be big or small.

If you notice you're getting in your head about this, tune in to your body. Drop your tailbone, sit back, and just let yourself draw.

Don't overthink it. Don't even think about it at all. You can think about your grocery list if you want. And every once in a while, just notice. *Okay, am I in my head about this? Am I thinking about what I should draw? Or am I just letting the drawing happen?*

If you know what you're drawing in advance, you're not doing it right. Get out of that knowing. Get out of that planning. Get out of that analyzing. That is a sign you're up in your head.

Let your tailbone drop and come back into the energy of play.

Step 3. Continue until the timer ends or your page is full.

Managing finances

Let's face it—we've all had moments where we thought, *Ugh, if I had more money, life would be easier!* And honestly, that's probably true. With more money comes more privilege, comes more opportunities. However, money itself isn't the answer to all our problems. The truth is, you can make twice the amount of money you do today and still feel like it's not enough. The difference is in your relationship to your finances.

Because of the negativity bias in your brain, you're always going to zoom in on the debt, bills, and lack of money you have. This can be all-consuming, and it is important to be aware of. If we get too fixated on this lack, though, we can feel frozen and stuck in our financial situation.

At the same time, you can also zoom out and see the myriad of ways abundance shows up in your life at any given moment. Maybe it's the dollar bill you found in your jacket pocket, the strawberries you were going to buy anyway ending up on sale, or getting an extra donut hole at the drive-thru.

By training your brain to seek abundance, you release the anxiety around money. Just for this breath, can you let go of the worry of not having enough? Just for this breath, can you see opportunities to resolve your debts? Just for this breath, can you tune in to the abundance all around you?

Remember: we ALL deserve to live abundant lives. It isn't greedy to ask the universe for abundance. When you have more money, you can give freely to charities, local businesses, friends, or families in need. When you spend money, you are supporting someone else's abundance, which comes back around to support your abundance.

As you move through these tasks, you may become aware of your own beliefs around money that impact your finances. Get curious when these come up. Are these beliefs helpful? Where did they come from? Are you ready to release them?

Abundance journal

This is my foolproof method for turning a scarcity mindset into an abundance mindset. Each day, write down three examples of abundance from your day. Let these be teeny tiny examples, like you found a quarter in your shoe or your favorite chips were buy one, get one half off. These examples don't have to be financial, either—abundance can come in many forms: abundance of energy, creativity, compliments, etc. What makes YOU feel abundant? Here are a few more examples:

- I made it to work today with plenty of time to settle in before the staff meeting.
- My favorite Netflix show released ten new episodes all at once.
- I used a coupon to buy my coffee.
- My boss bought us lunch.
- Four people liked my hair today.
- I felt motivated to finish my manuscript.

Your daily abundance journaling should take you two minutes or less. At first it may feel challenging to think of the examples, but after a few days you'll notice yourself clocking them in your daily life. Do this every day, and by the end of the week notice how your mindset has changed.

Abundance candle

Before we dive into each of the financial tasks, you'll want to set the stage for your new abundance mindset with a candle. Grab a seven-day pillar candle—green or purple is great for abundance, white is great to help heal your relationship to money, and black will help if you feel the need to protect your money.

On the outside of the candle, draw an abundance sigil, an affirmation of abundance, or a symbol that represents your local currency. If you want to get really fancy, add all three options! Now you can decorate your candle with herbs for abundance, crystals, oils, and anything else you have around your house.

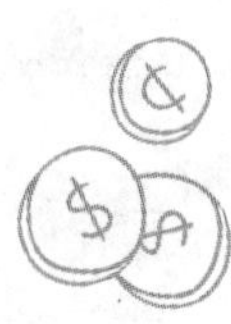

Place the candle on your altar or in a dedicated space. Underneath the candle, place a piece of paper currency or a voided check. When doing financial chores, light your candle and connect with the feeling of abundance.

Making money: abundance spells

Our relationship to abundance can be a sticky one—money often brings up feelings tied to anxiety, our self-worth, scarcity. Even our familial relationships and upbringing can create programming around money that holds us back from believing we are worthy of true abundance. The following meditation is one you may want to revisit a few times. Sometimes it can take a few tries to get that tension to dissolve, especially if you have a particularly difficult relationship with money to start. But keep at it, be patient, and be kind to yourself.

MEDITATION

Release Tension Around Money

Go ahead and lie down for this one. If it feels comfortable, you could lie on your back, or if you have an empty wall nearby, you could swing your legs up the wall.

Just really let yourself find comfort here. One of the things that happens whenever we start talking about abundance, working with abundance, is that there's this inherent tension or discomfort that comes with it. Just think about how conversations about money are uncomfortable in public or with people you don't know very well.

Even with people you do know well, there's this inherent discomfort built into our relationship with abundance.

So my invitation to you is to get as physically comfortable as possible to set the tone for this meditation. Reinforce this idea that you don't have to be uncomfortable with money.

You don't have to be physically uncomfortable.

You don't have to be emotionally uncomfortable.

You don't have to be energetically uncomfortable.

Let your physical posture set the tone for that; let yourself really sprawl out. If you want to, swaddle yourself in a blanket. Maybe rock the shoulders or the head, work out some of the tension in your neck. Give yourself a few more breaths to settle in and feel the parts of your body that are supported here.

Notice the physical support underneath you, under your legs, your feet, your hips, your spine, your head. See if you can melt into that physical support a little bit more.

As you breathe, can you feel the support behind your breath? Notice the support of your diaphragm, your lungs, all the muscles and tissues in your chest, your throat, your nostrils.

Recognize how physically supported you are. Right here, right now.

Next, bring into your awareness how you are emotionally supported right now. Become aware of something that brings you comfort. Maybe it's a blanket or a pet or a person—something that, when you're in its presence, you feel completely at ease or as close to it as possible.

Feel that support bubble up within your body, that emotional support.

Now, as you hold that emotional support in your body, can you feel all the energetic support around you?

Maybe you feel the different energies in your space, within your body.

Maybe you work with guides, or ancestors, or other forms of spiritual support.

Feel your body physically supported, that emotional support, and the energetic support all around you here.

You are so deeply supported.

Lean into this support on all layers as you bring into your awareness your relationship with money. Maybe you envision opening your bank account or your wallet, or any other symbol of abundance that calls to you.

Simply notice how your physical body responds to that relationship with money, with abundance. Has anything changed or shifted in the body? And if so, can you bring that energy of emotional support to that part?

And can you bring the physical support of your breath to any parts of your body that are holding tension around this relationship to money?

And as your awareness pools there, all of that energetic support pools there as well. Energy goes where your awareness goes, and you start to feel that tension dissolve.

Once again, feel yourself physically, emotionally, and energetically supported here.

Perhaps you start to acknowledge how your relationship with money is another form of support, holding hands with the physical, the emotional, and the energetic.

Once again, feel the support underneath you, under your feet, your legs, your hips.

Imagine any of that leftover tension could drain out the legs, out the feet, into the earth.

Take one more deep breath in here, then open your mouth to let it go.

Attracting abundance with money bowls

Money bowls are powerful abundance attractors and are easy to create using household ingredients. You'll want to cleanse your vessel and the items you're adding to it. Here's what you will need:

- **Vessel:** Grab a fun jar, plate, dish, or bowl. Any material, shape, color, or size is great. This is a really fun thrift store hunt to go on, or shop your stash of unused jars. (I know you have sixty-two waiting for a purpose in your cabinet right now!)

- **Base:** This will make up the bulk of your jar. You can use natural materials like sand, dirt, or rocks. Or you can use pantry staples like grains, dried legumes, oats, or rice. The latter is a great option if you have food items that your family doesn't enjoy eating or are about to expire—give them a new use in your money bowl!

- **Money:** Any denomination, cash or coin, works. You can even use Monopoly money or a voided check. I will often put in checks after I mobile deposit them. This acts as a magnet for more money to come your way.

- **Abundance attractors:** Herbs, spices, crystals, and other objects that attract abundance work well here. Check the Ingredients Appendix (page 291) for a full list of options and remember to use what you have on hand!

- **Extras:** Tarot cards, affirmations, sigils, jewelry—anything else you want to add to infuse the bowl with the energy of abundance!

Assembling your money bowl

Cleanse your vessel and other supplies with smoke or sound. To use sound, you can ring a bell over the top of your items, or simply clap or scream into the jar. Screaming can be very cathartic in addition to cleansing any stagnant energy!

Now add your base, with the intention of growing your financial foundation. Top with money to clarify your intention. Finally, add in your abundance attractors and anything else you want to decorate your money bowl!

Place your money bowl somewhere with reverence, avoiding spaces that get cluttered so there is a free flow of energy around your bowl. On the new moon or on your payday, feed your money bowl to keep it fresh and growing your abundance for you!

Money bowl maintenance

Feeding your money bowl is an offering of gratitude, a "Thank you; more please!" to keep the momentum going. You can feed your money bowl in various ways: by adding more of the abundance attractors you placed in before, offering your own energy by holding it in your hands and sending gratitude from your heart, or dropping a few coins from your pocket into the bowl.

Here are some things to sprinkle into your money bowl that work wonders:

- **Ground coffee** to speed up abundance
- **Cinnamon** for prosperity
- **Mint** for abundance
- **Catnip** to attract money
- **Lavender** to reduce stress around money
- **Cloves** to protect your finances
- **Garlic powder** to banish debts
- **Salt** for protection

Mix these ingredients up in a jar, label it with an abundance sigil or a dollar sign, then keep it near your money bowl to feed as needed.

When to refresh

Every so often you will want to do a full refresh of your money bowl. This is to help prevent your abundance from stagnating and to ensure the herbs don't go funky. Around the solstice or equinox, take your money and extras out of the bowl and give them a cleanse. Next, dispose of the base, offering a thank-you as you do so. Physically clean the bowl with soap and water, dry very well, then spiritually cleanse with sound or smoke and remake your money bowl!

You may notice that your relationship to money changes throughout the year, so the abundance attractors and extras may change with it. For instance, if you are feeling stressed about money, you may add herbs for stress relief. Or if you are feeling an abundance of money, you may have a crystal for gratitude in there next time you refresh it. Let the process be fun and explore what you want to add!

Budgeting

When it comes to calling in more abundance, getting specific can help you attract more money. What better way to get specific than by giving each of your dollars a job through a monthly budget? Grab a green or purple pen to represent abundance, light a candle adorned with an abundance sigil or your local currency symbol, and sit down to write out your budget. Start with how much you make per paycheck, then divide your budget into four categories: fixed expenses (like your mortgage, rent, day care, and utilities), variable expenses (like groceries and gas), extraneous expenses (like gifts, clothes, entertainment, restaurants), and savings (rainy-day fund, IRA, 401(k)). Make sure your paycheck covers the most important expenses before moving on to the extraneous expenses, and always set aside at least one dollar for savings.

Now make yourself a second budget, this time a dream budget. If money was no object, what would you actually spend it on? Would your rent change? Would you spend more on groceries? Upgrade your car? As you daydream about your ideals, notice where your priorities lie. If your first instinct was to upgrade your car, how can you begin setting aside a few extra dollars each month now to make that dream come true? Manifestation requires clarity but also action, so the priorities you set in your budget will help you get closer to your financial goals.

Revisit your budget often, lighting your abundance candle each time you sit down to do your finances. It's easy to get swept up in feeling you'll never have enough money, so starting to reframe your relationship to finances will help you experience more abundant feelings and less scarcity. Begin by recognizing that, even if you put only one dollar toward savings, your abundance is, in fact, growing.

Paying bills

Paying bills can become a practice of gratitude. When was the last time you lost power or running water? Can you recall how grateful you felt when it returned? As you pay each bill, consider repeating statements of gratitude for the thing you are paying for. For example:

- I am grateful for my car because it gets me safely around town.
- I am grateful for electricity so I can read late into the night.
- I am grateful for the internet and all the ways it connects me to my loved ones.
- I am grateful for my credit card because it allows me to provide for my family.
- I am grateful for Netflix and all the fun movie nights we've had with the kids.

If you're struggling to come up with a gratitude statement, it may be a sign your priorities have shifted. Take some time to revisit your budget and reallocate those funds to something more beneficial, if you are able to.

Decreasing screen time

We're all addicted to our phones these days—you're not alone! These devices and their apps are literally designed to stimulate chemicals in our brains that make us want to keep coming back for more. The antidote to this is mindfulness. Becoming aware of when and why we use these devices will help you break the cycle of mindless scrolling.

To begin, consider using a screen time tracking app. Perhaps your phone already has one installed. You need to know where you are before you can create change. Log your screen time for a week without trying to change anything. Awareness is the first step of mindfulness.

Next, build in mindfulness breaks. You can set screen time limits on your phone or download an app like One Sec that will create mindfulness breaks for you. If you can, change the wording on your limits to say something like, "Take a deep breath before you scroll." Each time the screen time notification comes up, stop to notice how you are feeling and ask yourself if you wish to continue on your phone.

Disable notifications for your social media and other apps that suck you down the scroll hole. Enable notifications for your meditation apps, water reminder apps, and other apps that force you to check in with yourself.

Be gentle with yourself as you break this cycle of digital addiction—mindfulness requires compassionate awareness, not judgment.

Finally, each week check back in with your screen time tracker and make adjustments. Notice when you become critical of your progress, and repeat statements of loving-kindness instead.

Purging negative energy from your digital space

The internet and social media can be a place where negative energy festers, but it can also be a beautiful place of connection and community. If you feel like your experience online has been skewing more negative than positive, it's time to purge the negative energy from your digital space. Try the following meditation.

MEDITATION

Clear and Shield Your Digital Space

Hold your phone between your hands and close your eyes. Imagine clear, bright energy flowing from the universe around you into the crown of your head. If you practice Reiki, you can invite Reiki energy to flow as well. Allow that clear energy to move down your head to your heart, filling it with the intention of kindness and connection.

Allow that energy to flow down your arms, then out of your hands, into your phone, and into your digital space. See or feel your online profiles filled with this light, banishing any darkness or negativity.

As this energy flows, imagine it continuing to pour out of your phone into the space around you, filling the room you are in, your building, the community around you, eventually covering the entire planet.

With this expansive light flowing through and around you, invite anyone who wishes to connect with your digital space through kindness to find you, and ask this light to cloak you from anyone who wishes to cause harm or spread hatred so they cannot enter your digital space.

Feel the light come back to your body, settling in your heart space. Take a deep breath in and exhale out your mouth.

Remembering passwords

Create a digital grimoire and use it to remember your passwords. A grimoire, sometimes called a Book of Shadows, is essentially a recipe book for your spells. Your digital grimoire can be on your computer or stored in the cloud as a document. In your protection rituals section, write down your protection sigils and record your passwords. Keep it safe and protected physically as well.

Passwords themselves can become spells. Remember that affirmations become more powerful when used often. So why not turn your passwords into an affirmation?

"I am powerful" could become "I@mP0werful!"

"I love unconditionally" can turn into "*IL0v3unc0nd!tion@lly*"

"I am financially free" can be written as "F!n@nci@l_Freed0m$$"

Using different characters, numbers, and symbols while using a phrase for your password also increases security. Making each site a different password improves security further, and affirmations can help you keep track of them all—perhaps your banking login uses an affirmation for abundance, your email login could use an affirmation for kind communication, your social media could use a phrase for protection, and so on.

Deep Magic

Taxes

We often see paying taxes as a negative, but what if you turned it into a celebration of abundance? As you sit down to do your quarterly or annual taxes, tune in to how you've spent money this year.

How did the money flow to you and where did you spend it? How did your spending impact your community?

Think about the local businesses you supported and how each dollar spent created a ripple effect to support the rest of your community, ultimately making a circular experience of abundance as the money flows back to you. See all the ways your tax dollars have improved your community, infrastructure, schools, and green spaces. See how, even though you spend money, you also receive abundance in other ways. Can you feel how you are always connected to the abundance that is all around you?

If you need to write a check for taxes owed, feel how this abundance will cycle through your local and national communities. Think about the people and places you will be impacting by making this payment, and the ways it comes back around to you eventually.

If you receive a tax refund, how can you celebrate this abundance returning to you? Perhaps you consciously decide to shop at a local small business and imagine the ripple effect you're creating for their abundance.

Taking paid time off

You deserve to rest. Period. There are likely a lot of voices in your head saying otherwise, from your boss to the media to the capitalistic ideas planted within you from a young age. But know that without rest, you cannot create. Without rest, you cannot expand. Without rest, you cannot reach your full potential.

If you're struggling to take your (well-deserved) paid time off, consider this variation of a loving-kindness practice.

Place your hand to your heart and repeat the following phrases in your mind:

- I deserve to be safe.
- I deserve to be happy.
- I deserve to be healthy.
- I deserve to be at peace.
- I deserve to rest.
- I deserve to take this time for myself.

Now submit your PTO request and enjoy it. (Don't you dare let me catch you checking your inbox on those days off, either!)

Job hunting

Sending off a job application is like casting a petition into the universe for the type of career you want. Here's a spell for finding a job listing, applying for it, and nailing your interview.

Before you even begin scrolling the job postings, light your abundance candle. Take a few moments to breathe and imagine the career you want. What would you wear? What time would you wake up? What do you eat for lunch? Write down all the details.

Now, each day as you hunt for this job, live your life as if it's already yours. Set your alarm for the time you would need to wake up for this ideal job. Dress for the job you want—bet you've heard that before, but it really does help you manifest to physically walk in the shoes of who you are becoming!

As you scroll the job postings, notice which listings stick out to you as you stay connected to this new version of yourself you're manifesting. When you spruce up your résumé, consider adding a hidden sigil to it! Make a sigil for career success, draw it in transparent ink or white, and place it in the background of your résumé. Or, if you're not super tech-savvy, draw it with your finger over your résumé before sending it off to your future employers.

Before your interview, repeat affirmations for confidence. Since you've been living in your future self's shoes for a while now, you'll automatically feel more confident when you walk into the interview.

Promotion spells

Just like in the job-hunting spell, you can begin to manifest a promotion by changing your routines and the way you dress. Consider the version of you who has already been promoted: What do they look like? What do they wear? What's their morning routine? Start to implement these things into your life now.

Here's a big caveat—if the promotion you want comes with a hefty pay raise, do not fall into the trap of spending money you do not have as you try to become this version of yourself. You can be this person without the money. Instead of buying a new wardrobe, focus on the smaller things: How do you take your coffee in the morning? What do you listen to on your commute? How do you wind down on the weekends? Let yourself live as the version of yourself who has achieved the promotion, then watch how easily you climb the career ladder!

Organizing your computer desktop

Let's make a digital altar to inspire you to keep your desktop organized! Just like your physical space, your digital space holds energy that impacts you physically and emotionally. You'll want to use some kind of art software for this. I'm a big fan of using Canva for easy drag-and-drop creation, but you can use whatever software you are comfortable with.

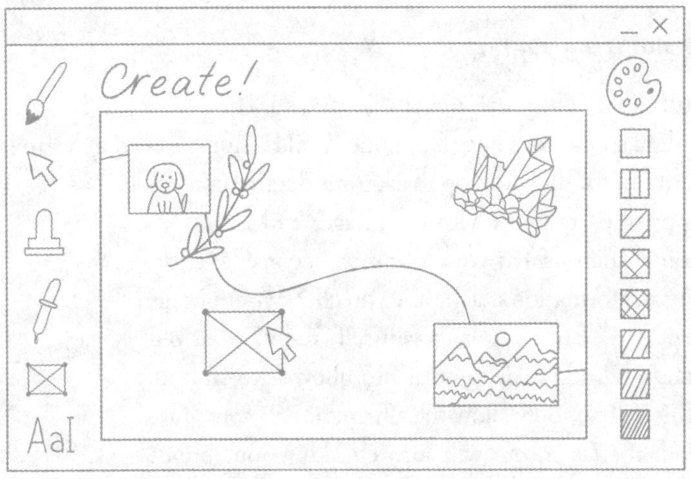

Begin with a blank canvas the size of your desktop—what energy do you want to invite into your digital space? Paint the canvas that color based on the Color Magic chart on page 45 in Chapter 2 or based on your own color associations.

Now begin to build a vision board for your work: What images inspire you? What images do you aspire to become? Add these to your canvas. Save room around these images to put your folders and necessary files.

Then add ingredients to amplify your intentions. Add artwork or images of herbs, crystals, images that correspond to the elements, energetic protections, sigils, deities—whatever feel supportive to you!

Finally, set your digital altar as your background, arranging your folders and files so that they add to the altar and ensure that it stays uncluttered and intentional.

When you notice your desktop becoming disorganized, it's time to refresh your altar! Begin again from scratch or edit your existing altar to feel more aligned with your needs and goals.

Organizing your apps

Just as we did for the digital altar on your computer, you can create a digital altar for your cell phone. Build a home screen in a similar fashion to the desktop background, arranging your apps to correspond with the images and intentions you've laid out. For your lock screen, consider creating an affirmation. Each time you check your phone, repeat the affirmation to yourself internally or out loud and take a deep breath to allow it to sink in. This will not only allow the affirmation to come into your life faster, but will turn checking your phone into a mindfulness cue to make you more aware of your habits around screen time and checking notifications.

You can also use affirmations to organize your apps. Create folders for your apps and label them with an affirmation—for instance, your banking and finance apps could be labeled "I am abundant," while your social media apps could be labeled "I am connected." This is also a great manifestation technique—use an affirmation of something you want to manifest and add the relevant apps to that folder. For example, when I was manifesting working for myself, I labeled all my business-related apps with "I am self-employed."

Purging old contacts

Did you know that your personality is reflective of the people you surround yourself with? Therefore, the people in your life have a direct impact on who you are and who you will become. Do the people you surround yourself with bring you closer to the version of yourself you are manifesting? Do they uplift your energy? Or are you keeping some people around that act as anchors, weighing you down?

As an equinox or solstice ritual, reflect on the energies of the people you have around you. Scroll through your contacts and determine if there are any anchors weighing down your phone book without reason. Delete the people you have no desire to have in your life anymore in order to make space for uplifting energy. When you come across someone who does uplift you but you haven't spoken to in a while, send them a note of gratitude or a quick hello to reconnect with their energy.

Organizing your camera roll

Set this as a full moon ritual. Each full moon, spend an hour or less going through the previous month's photos. Reflect on your month with gratitude as you review the moments you deemed worthy of capturing. Some photos (or screenshots) may have felt poignant at the time but now feel unnecessary. Release the energy of those moments by deleting them. Finally, choose a few images that sum up how this last month has made you feel and save them to a designated folder. At the end of the year, reflect on these moments with gratitude and consider journaling on the growth you've experienced each month.

Chapter 9

Miscellaneous Rooms

You may have spaces in your home that aren't covered in the previous chapters—in which case you will likely find them here. Remember: even the smallest nooks and crannies deserve to be infused with Magic! In contrast to the other chapters, structured by type of Magic, this one is organized by room. So take what you need here and skip over the rooms that don't pertain to you.

Kids' Room

Getting kids involved with Mundane Magic can be a powerful tool to empower your kiddos to take responsibility for their space while also strengthening their sense of autonomy. Consider teaching your children to practice gratitude for their toys as they put them away, or to choose their clothing for school based on Color Magic and what intention they feel they need each day. Remind them that their energy belongs to them, and teach them to tune in to their energy while tidying up their room—ask them how the space feels before versus after. This demonstrates to your child that they have the right to feel safe and comfortable in their own space. It also allows them to strengthen their intuition muscle, which can come in handy and keep them safer as they grow!

Nightmare banishing

If your child suffers from nightmares, enlist their help to create a nightmare-banishing ritual. For this, you'll need a spray bottle, some salt, and an essential oil or fragrance oil of their choosing. Gently heat the water in the microwave to dissolve the salt. Allow your child to stir the salt into the water, counterclockwise to banish any nightmares or monsters, clockwise to invite in peaceful sleep. Each night, allow your child to spray under their bed and anywhere else the monsters hide while stating out loud, "This is MY space—no monsters can come in without my permission!" Feel free to adapt the statement to fit your child's words, or have them write their own. The intention here is to allow your child to set the tone for the energy of their space.

If your child prefers to sleep with a night-light, consider introducing the concept of a "ghost light" to them. In the theater, there's a tradition that a light is always left on when the theater is dark to help guide helpful, benevolent spirits to the production and keep away any that may wish to cause harm. We can use this intention with night-lights—while the light is on, unwelcome entities and spirits must stay away.

Cleaning kids' toys

Your kiddo is constantly growing and outgrowing their toys and belongings. But they likely have that one stuffie that they love regardless of how grimy it may get. Consider teaching your child how to cleanse the energy of their toys—let them know that when you wash their stuffie, only unwanted energies get washed away, like dirt, germs, and grime. But all the love and happy energy sticks around. Invite your child to wash the unwanted energy away from their toys regularly after cleaning—have your child send love back into the toy by giving it a hug!

When your child has outgrown a toy, encourage them to place it in a donation box with a statement of gratitude or a wish that the toy find a home better fit for them. Teach your child that giving away toys they won't play with anymore gives another child the opportunity to enjoy their toy instead. Let them send the toy off with even more loving energy.

Sorting clothes

Sorting clothing can be a fun opportunity to let your child tune in to their energetic needs. Instead of asking them, "Does this fit?," ask them, "Does this make you feel strong? Confident? Happy?" As your child tunes in to their emotions, they begin to build associations between their emotions and their clothing. This is the same as setting an intention and forming connections using Color Magic! Your child will begin to feel that energy of confidence when they pop on their Spider-Man shirt or their purple socks, giving them space to recognize emotions and reinforce their energetic autonomy.

Collecting and purging kids' artwork

Your kids make A LOT of art, and you can't possibly store it all! Instead of creating a giant pile or drawer full of artwork you'll never get to enjoy, get your kids involved in displaying their art! Pick up a shadow box frame and hang it somewhere in your home. As your child brings home artwork, place it in the frame for storage. Every week, ask your child what their intention is for the week—have them choose a piece of artwork that matches that intention and place it at the front of the frame to display. If no artwork fits their intention, encourage them to create something new. Each night at the dinner table, encourage your child to reflect on their intention and share their Magic moment of the week. This allows your child to get more deeply in touch with their feelings, encourages conversation and reflection, and keeps their intention top of mind throughout the week.

Basement or Attic

The creepy-crawly spaces of your home need love, too! I used to live in a hundred-year-old house with a very damp, stinky basement. Anytime we opened the door, our entire house smelled dank. Turns out, a basement like that can actually affect the air quality of the entire house! Your house is like a sandwich, and the rooms we've covered so far are the cheese, condiments, and lettuce of the sandwich. What's the most crucial ingredient? The bread. Without that, the sandwich falls apart. Energetically, your basement and attic are like the bread of your home—they sandwich the energy in your entire house, they are the barrier between your home's energy and the energy outside your home, and the energetic flow in these spaces impacts the overall energy of your home. So don't disregard the basement or attic!

Clearing cobwebs

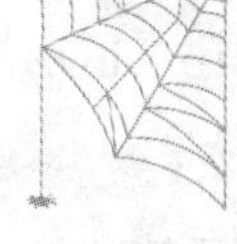

Cobwebs can represent entanglement—they are created haphazardly and can appear more often when the mind is confused, hazy, or obscured. If you've been needing clarity on a specific situation, consider clearing the cobwebs of your mind by removing cobwebs from your home. As you sweep away each cobweb, take some deep breaths and release the clutter of your mind.

Bugs and pests

Let's face it: one of the worst parts about the basement or attic are all the bugs and other pests you may encounter. While Magic may not be able to cure your fear of these little creatures, seeing an unexpected critter in your home can be a spiritual message in disguise.

In the following chart, read through the symbolism for the pest you've found in your home and see if it resonates with your life right now. Perhaps when you encounter the next creepy-crawly thing, your fear will be dampened by the message it is sharing with you.

BUG/INSECT/PEST	SPIRITUAL SYMBOLISM
Ant	Teamwork, unity, cooperation
Bat	Rebirth, end of a cycle, transformation
Bee	Harmony, community, prosperity
Centipede	Change, grounding, healing
Cockroach	Strength, abundance, survival
Cricket	Self-expression, intuition, luck
Earwig	Letting go, transformation, growth
Flea	Rebirth, change, introspection
Gnat	Persistence, resilience, need for cleansing
Housefly	Change, development, decision making
Ladybug	Luck, renewal, healing
Mosquito	Protection, perseverance, renewal
Moth	Resurrection, vulnerability, wisdom
Mouse	Courage, resourcefulness, wit
Possum	Harmony, transformation, survival
Rat	Opportunity, prosperity, wisdom
Scorpion	Protection, solitude, independence
Silverfish	Adaptability, resilience, change
Skunk	Confidence, protection, balance
Snake	Transformation, letting go, protection
Spider	Interconnectedness, patience, manifestation
Squirrel	Organization, problem solving, adaptability
Stinkbug	Protection, grounding, spiritual awakening
Termite	Hard work, letting go/release, speed
Tick	Tenacity, purification, need for rest
Wasp	Discipline, luck, transformation

Removing bugs from your furry friends

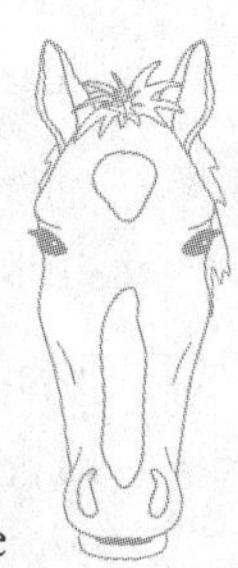

We never want bugs to bother our furry friends. But when they do, and you have to pull them off or bathe your pet with special soap, you might as well make it Magical. For bugs you need to manually remove such as ticks, set the intention that the tick take away any harmful or negative energy as it is removed. For bugs you need to bathe away, cleanse the energy using soap and water, as described in the bathing pets section of Chapter 6 on bathrooms (page 172).

Emptying the dehumidifier

As your basement dehumidifier collects water, it's also collecting energy that exists in the space. As the container fills, it is a physical representation of how clear the energy in your space is becoming. Think about the feeling of a damp, humid basement versus your basement after the dehumidifier has run for a while—the air feels lighter, easier to breathe. This is a great opportunity to become familiar with how energy feels when it's cleansed versus stagnant. As you empty your dehumidifier, reflect on how the space feels in your body. How does the air feel to breathe? How does the basement feel to be in? As you dump the contents, express gratitude for this device keeping the energy clear for you.

Catchall Rooms

These random odds-and-ends rooms can become collection points for clutter and therefore energy. I know, for my own home, the more chaotic my schedule is, the more chaotic my mudroom becomes and suddenly we start leaving our shoes and jackets in the kitchen and living room. But when my mudroom is organized, our shoes and jackets have a home, meaning that clutter and chaos don't leak out into the rest of our space. So keeping these areas clear can help the rest of your home feel more spacious.

Closets

A cluttered closet is the perfect place for stagnant energy to hide, so going through the clutter naturally helps open up the energy of your home for greater flow. Not to mention, if your closet is sorted, you won't have to worry, say, about buying yet another roll of wrapping paper even though you already have seventeen rolls tucked into the back of your closet. Whether your coat closet holds coats or a little bit of everything, try this Mundane Magic to clear the energy AND your clutter.

Start by taking out from that closet the things you actually use on a regular basis. If you don't use anything regularly, shut the door and ignore it. (Kidding, kind of.) Sorting the items by how often you utilize them and putting the least-used items in the very back of the closet will make it easier to keep the energy flowing in this space.

Now give everything a good cleanse—the easiest way is to use smoke or sound to do this. For smoke, burn some incense and run the smoke over your items. For sound, ring a bell or shake that jingle bell you found in the random pile of holiday decorations; you can play music from your phone as well. If you want to do a deeper cleanse, consider washing any items that can go in the washer and setting the rest out in the sun for a few hours.

As you bring each item back into the closet, start with the items you use least. Tuck those in the back, but as you do, use this as an exercise to strengthen your intuition. Is this something you need? Does its energy support you or your home? If so, tuck it into the back of the closet. If not, consider donating it.

As you get to the items you use most often, be sure they are as accessible as possible in the closet. This will ensure you remove them often as you use them, which allows the energy to keep flowing in this space.

Mudroom

Your mudroom (or wherever your shoes and jackets live) is one of the thresholds of energy in your home. Your jackets, shoes, and keys hold a tremendous amount of energy from all the places you go and all the people you encounter.

If you're anything like me, your mudroom is a catchall space of junk. So first things first, move the items that don't belong there back to their home. (For a guided "Clutter-Crushing Charm" meditation, flip to page 70 in Chapter 3.) This will free up the energy in this space so you can clear out any unwanted energy before it enters your home.

As you tidy your mudroom, consider cleansing the energy in the space. One way to do this is by leaving a spray bottle of moon water in the room and spritzing your shoes, purses, jackets, and reusable grocery bags as they reenter the home.

If you have a mat or boot tray in your mudroom, consider drawing a cleansing sigil on it (on top or underneath) to cleanse your shoes as they enter your home.

Now, the items in your mudroom are also totems to protect your energy when you are out and about—consider writing a protection sigil on a slip of paper and keeping it in your jacket pocket. Draw a protection sigil on the inside of your shoes and grocery bags—use clear nail polish if you want to be stealthy about it.

Home Renovations and Building Maintenance

A fresh coat of paint is like adding fresh energy to a space—if you've ever painted a room that felt drab, you've experienced this! Anytime you do maintenance to your home, you are maintaining the energy in your home. Think of it like the paint on your walls—when the paint becomes scuffed, dirty, or even chipped, so does the energy in that room. Often the paint is what shows the age of the room, and a fresh coat can really spruce up the space. It's the same thing with energy—when you do a renovation (big or small!) or maintenance to the house, you are making sure the energy stays fresh and vibrant in the home.

Painting (touch-ups and whole walls)

Before you begin painting, draw sigils on your walls to invite an intention into the space. You can draw these sigils with a pen or with the paint itself before rolling it on the walls. When you're finished painting, draw the sigil on the paint to remember and connect with the same intention for touch-ups.

If there's a specific energy you'd like to call into your home, use Color Magic to decide what color to paint your front door. If there's a specific intention you'd like to set for a space, use Color Magic to help you choose a shade. For instance, paint blue accents in the dining room to encourage peaceful conversations over dinner or yellow in the laundry room to motivate you to fold your clothes!

Hanging frames and photos

Hanging decorations can set the theme of your space and therefore influence the energy of your home. Have you ever gone into a restaurant bathroom that was highly decorated and it influenced the conversation at your table when you returned to the meal? This is one example of how wall decor can change the energy of your space and influence how your family and guests interact in your home. For instance, one of the bathrooms in our home is themed around naval history (it's named the *head,* where you go to take a "*ship*"); in it, there's a framed portrait of a ship named *Fanny,* among other decor to suit the theme. It's always a surprise to folks when they use this bathroom, but they always come back to the living room smiling.

As you choose decor for your walls, get some inspiration by asking yourself, *How will this influence the energy in this space? What reactions do I want people to have?* If you have a family that struggles to communicate around the dinner table, perhaps you hang more detailed art in that room to give everyone something to talk about. Because how you do anything is how you do everything, if the art in the room inspires folks to pick up on more intricate details, they may be more inclined to speak about some of the smaller details of their day. This one is great for those teenagers who answer your questions about school with one-word answers!

Changing air filters

This is a great equinox or solstice ritual to help purify the energy of your home for the new season. When you change the filter, consider drawing a sigil on the new filter to set an intention for your home. As the air flows through the filter, the intention of your sigil can move through your home. This is a great opportunity to connect with the other members in your home to set a communal intention. What does your family wish to focus on this season? Where is your energy being directed already? What intention can you call in for support with your goals?

Perhaps you choose an intention based on the season—autumn is a great time to release and let go of anything draining your energy. Here are a few intentions to consider based on the seasons—but feel free to go off script and make your own!

SEASON	SUGGESTED INTENTIONS
Spring	**Rebirth and creation:** As seedlings start poking through the soil, we begin to sow and cultivate seeds of our future. What do you want to create this year? What energies will support you in calling this in?
Summer	**Growth and gratitude:** The sun's rays invite us to expend energy and create even more momentum toward our goals. Turn your attention outward toward your community and nature itself. How can you foster a feeling of connection during these months? What has grown in your life this year that you can express gratitude toward?

SEASON	SUGGESTED INTENTIONS
Autumn	**Release and letting go:** Just as the trees drop their leaves to conserve energy for the winter hibernation, you're invited to release that which is draining your energy. What is holding you back from resting? What are you ready to let go?
Winter	**Conservation and hibernation:** As the plants go dormant, so does our energy. This is the time to turn inward, take inventory of how you're spending your energy, and rest in anticipation for the spring season ahead.

Smoke and carbon monoxide detectors

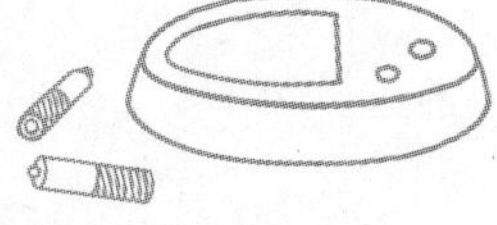

Your detectors are protection spells in the most literal sense. Consider pressing the button and testing them on the new moon to protect your manifestations as they come into your life. Draw a protection sigil on them, or in the battery compartment if you want to be stealthy. Once a year, depending on the type of detector you use, change the batteries—I prefer to do this around the spring equinox because that is the time for planting seeds for the new year. But if it's been a while, do it right now.

Home repairs

Say it with me now: "How you do anything is how you do EVERYTHING." If you have a list of simple home repairs you could do but keep putting them off, now is the time to look at where in your emotional life you're doing the same.

Have a tough conversation you know you need to have AND

need to clean the fridge coils? Maybe you have been procrastinating on starting a new healthy habit and you need to repaint your deck? Those cables under the TV you keep saying you'll take care of might reflect the stretches your physical therapist gave you that you keep "forgetting" to do.

Use one to motivate the other—as you do this small repair task, ask the fresh energy you are calling into your home to clear out obstacles in the way of tackling your other to-dos.

Chapter 10

Yard and Outside the Home

The space around your home is the energetic barrier between your house and the rest of the world. Just as a fence (or a moat) prevents people and animals from waltzing into your lawn, the protective energy around your home prevents unwanted energy from waltzing into your home. That is, when the protective energy is maintained properly. Let's explore some chores outside the home through this lens of Protection Magic.

Daily Rituals

Leaving the house. Period.

If you're sensitive to other people's energy, you might find it difficult to even leave your house. I get it, as someone who becomes easily overstimulated in crowded environments and doesn't like to leave the cozy cocoon that is my couch. Staying home always feels easier. However, we need to leave the house from time to time, and to do so gracefully requires a certain degree of Protection Magic. The following is a really good meditation to practice at home. Then, when you are out and about—say, at a concert or in a really crowded store—and you feel your energy start to become overwhelmed, you can come back to feeling that support of the earth and expanding your energy field to help push other people's energy away from you.

Try this meditation out and notice how you feel about leaving the house after.

MEDITATION

Energy Protection to Leave the House

Go ahead and get comfortable. Wherever you are, just place your feet on the floor there. You could be standing; you could be sitting. Really feel that connection between your feet and the earth.

As you start to connect with your feet, feel the muscles in your legs start to soften. A lot of times we hold tension in our glutes and the calves or in the lower back. See if you can just let that dissolve into the earth, into that support.

Take a deep breath in, then exhale out any stagnant energy, any energy that's not yours that you might be carrying right now.

I want you to imagine the energy field around your body, like a container of energy that separates you from the people around you. Imagine that this space is like an invisible balloon.

As you breathe in, draw in energy from the earth.

And as you exhale, let that balloon expand.

And as it expands, it becomes more firm. Your breath is fortifying that balloon, just like when we inflate a balloon; it becomes more rigid.

So inhaling, the support of the earth.

Exhaling, expanding that balloon, strengthening that energy field.

Do this a few more times on your own. Keep relaxing the leg muscles. Soften the shoulders.

Now come back to your natural effortless breath. And see if you can still feel that protective support around you.

As you leave your house—whether for work, the grocery store, Disney World, wherever you're going—just imagine you are surrounded by this bubble. Feel everyone else's energy just bounce off of your balloon.

Take one more deep breath in, open your mouth, and let it go. When you're ready, open your eyes.

Walking the dog

Walking is an amazing opportunity to shake off stress and stagnant energy. It can sometimes be hard to motivate yourself to get out the door, but making it Magical can help! Did you know that dogs relieve stress by sniffing? Especially in new environments, dogs will sniff for a while outside to decrease their fear response. Funnily enough, you can quiet your own stress by taking a sniff walk, too! Your brain is primed for survival, so taking a moment to really soak in your senses can quiet the stress response in your brain and nervous system.

As you take your dog on a walk, let them be your mindfulness cue. When they stop to sniff, take a moment to breathe the environment in with a deep breath. Take a look around, really absorbing the colors and shapes around you. If they start to pull, use this as an opportunity to cue them to mindfulness, take a breath, and pause the walk. Whether you go around the block or on a mile-long hike, allow your walk to calm your senses and bring you back to the Magic of the present moment.

Picking up poop

As the owner of two dogs, one of which seems to poop about seventy-two times a day, I can empathize with how annoying it is to pick up dog poop. Shifting your perspective may help make this stinky job a little less . . . well, stinky.

See each turd as an opportunity to express gratitude for your furry friend. As you prepare the bag, call in the feeling of appreciation and love you have for your pet. When you pick up the poop, repeat an affirmation of gratitude for them. Shifting your focus from the poop your pet creates to the love they create within you will make this task much more enjoyable!

Refilling bird feeders and cleaning birdbaths

Turn your bird-watching hobby into a manifestation ritual! As you clean the bird feeder and birdbath, imagine cleansing stagnant energy holding you back from achieving your manifestation. Refill the bird food in the feeder with the intention of feeding your desires and taking action toward your goals. As you watch the birds enjoy a meal, see your manifestations begin to take flight in your own life. Let the birds inspire you that just as they effortlessly stumbled upon their dinner, the things that are meant for you in this life will arrive at the perfect time with ease.

Magical Upkeep

Shoveling snow

Use your time shoveling snow to banish someone or something from your space. Perhaps you have a nagging inner monologue telling you that you won't achieve something, or there's someone who just won't quit bugging you. As you shovel the snow, repeat the affirmation, "May this snow freeze [person's behavior or thought pattern] from my space." Clear the pathways of your home as you clear this unwanted energy from your mind and body, clarifying your boundaries in the process.

Scraping the windshield

This is a great practice for getting clarity on a situation. Say you are having trouble seeing past an obstacle in your life or struggling to see another person's perspective, thus causing communication issues. As you scrape your windshield, repeat the affirmation, "As

I remove this ice from my windshield, I remove that which is blocking me from seeing [situation] clearly." When you reenter your car, gaze out the windshield with a beginner's mind of the situation—what aspects of this have you not looked at before?

Salting the walkway

This is the ultimate protection ritual for the winter season. As you salt or sand your walkway, repeat the affirmation, "May this [salt/sand] block unwanted energies and visitors from entering my home. And may it clear a safe pathway for the energies and people who I do want to visit me." Notice who walks up your front walkway with ease and who slips on the way.

Raking leaves

Whether you pile them up, mow them, or burn them, removing leaves from your yard is a Magical opportunity to release and let go of the things that no longer serve you. Just as the trees release their leaves to conserve energy for growth, we often have thought patterns, habits, and behaviors that stifle our growth. On the full moon or autumn equinox, make a list of things you're ready to release. Now, as you pick up your leaves, use this as an opportunity to let the items on that list go. Add your list to the bag of leaves or burn pile and use your yard as a visual reminder that you're ready to let go.

Mowing the lawn

Your lawn is like an energetic shield around your home. Whether you have a fenced-in yard or not, the lawn stands between your space and the public space of the road or sidewalks. Therefore, we can see tending to the lawn as an act of protection and warding for the space. Whether you like to trim your grass regularly or leave it to grow wild and support your local pollinators, caring for the green space around your home will help protect the energy inside your home.

Additionally, you can turn the scent of fresh-cut grass into a mindfulness cue—as you cut the lawn, take a deep breath in and mentally offer gratitude to your lawn for protecting your home. As you exhale, say thank you.

Gardening

The prolific spiritual teacher, peace activist, and Buddhist monk Thich Nhat Hanh teaches that we have a garden in our mind—with every thought we either plant seeds of peace, joy, and love or we plant seeds of hate, anger, and greed. Because how you do anything is how you do everything, we can use the physical act of gardening as a way to till the garden within our mind.

As you watch your garden grow, see this as a visual representation of the new thoughts and habits you are forming within yourself. Bonus—if you're growing an herb garden, you can use these herbs to imbue foods with this intention. Or if you're growing flowers, consider adding some cut flowers to your altar to represent your own spiritual growth.

Weeding

What seeds are you currently planting in your mind with your thoughts? What thoughts are you ready to release? As you pull each weed, mentally affirm the opposite of that thought. For example, if your thought is *I hate weeding,* instead mentally affirm, *I am so grateful to have this garden.* If your thought is *I am not good enough,* mentally affirm, *I am inherently worthy.*

Trimming and pruning

Just as cutting back a plant allows the plant to grow bigger and stronger, sometimes we face circumstances in life that feel like we are moving in the opposite direction of our goals. As you trim your garden, consider experiences in your recent past that have felt this way: How has this setback helped to accelerate your growth? Where can you plant the seeds of gratitude for this setback in the garden of your mind?

Mulching

When plants are fresh and tender, they must be protected. The same can be said for the new seeds you're planting in your mind. As you spread mulch over your garden, consider how you can continue to tend to these seeds in your daily life. Commit yourself to one action each day—maybe it's a gratitude journal, or a Mundane Magic task, or an affirmation before bed. As you tuck your plants in with the mulch, tuck your new mental seeds in with a promise of action.

Coiling the garden hose

Finally, after watering your seeds, it's time to put away the hose. As you detangle any kinks in the hose, imagine you are untangling any negative habit that could hold you back from this new growth you are establishing in your mind. With each coil of the hose, reaffirm your mental seedlings with affirmations of gratitude.

Deep Magic

Entryway cleaning

Your entryway or front porch is the energetic threshold of your space. The more items, dust, spiderwebs, and such that accumulate here, the more cluttered the energy will feel. This can create a bottleneck for anyone entering your home. It will be difficult for fresh, supportive energy to enter your home, and likewise stagnant energy can be blocked from leaving. Additionally, you can use your entryway to set energetic boundaries for your space.

Create a consistent routine of tidying up and cleansing your entryway—this is a great new moon or full moon routine! Cleaning the space will clear that bottleneck of energy, and it's a great opportunity to refresh any protection spells you're using for your home.

Protection rituals for your entryway:

- Draw a sigil for protection in chalk under your doormat.
- While we're at it, get a doormat that says something other than WELCOME. If you want to practice intentionally protecting your home, words matter. Protection rituals filter the energy that is welcome in your home—so if you DO choose a mat that says WELCOME, be sure to include some form of protection with it.
- Wash your front door with a mopping potion for protection (see Mopping Potions in the appendix, page 287).
- Place salt on the threshold or under the doormat.
- Paint your front door white, black, or red for protection.

- Grow rosemary next to your front door or walkway (potted pothos plants set inside the front door work, too).
- Create a sigil for your home using your address and draw it in clear nail polish on your front door.
- Keep black tourmaline with your house keys.
- Place a bell on your front door or doorknob to cleanse the energy coming in and out of your home.
- Keep a broom by your front door—bonus if it's a cinnamon broom! (See more tips on the following page.)
- Add protective crystals or herbs to your front door wreath.
- Add selenite and black tourmaline above your door frame and windows to protect the energy entering your space.

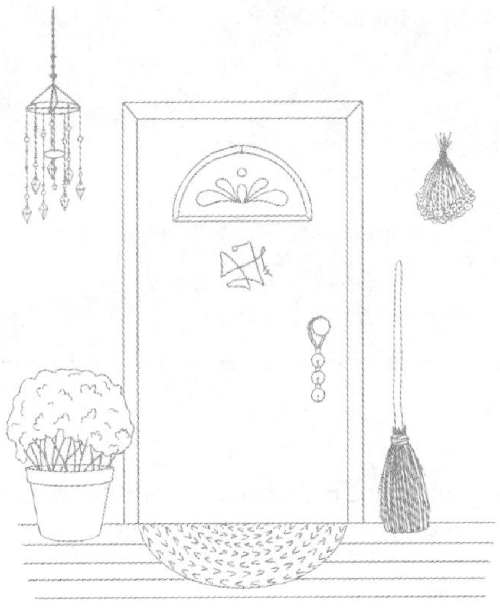

Cinnamon brooms

One of my personal favorite ways to influence the energy of the home is with cinnamon brooms! These are often found in grocery stores in the autumn months—you can find full-size or mini versions of these brooms, or make your own by binding pine needles together with string and adding a few drops of cinnamon essential oil. Cinnamon brooms are fantastic for warding and protecting your space, but also for inviting in luck, abundance, and prosperity. Here are a few Magical ways to use them:

- Keep one with the handle down by the front door to ward off unwanted guests.
- Face the handle up to invite in positive energy.
- Keep a mini cinnamon broom in your car or office to protect the energy.
- Sweep energy out the front door with the broom to cleanse and protect the energy of your house.
- Sweep energy with the broom into your front door to invite in abundance and prosperity.
- Use a mini cinnamon broom to sweep your altar for luck.
- Place a mini cinnamon broom with the handle facing up inside your money bowl to reenforce and protect your abundance.
- Decorate your cinnamon broom with the seasons! Add flowers for the spring equinox or bells and holly for the winter holidays.

- Hold your cinnamon broom during meditation to deepen your practice and for astral travel.

Cleaning out the garage

The energy of your garage is the transition between your personal and public life. It is very easy for energy to stagnate here, especially if your garage is a dumping ground for clutter. Instead, think of your garage as a transition from the hectic outside activities like work or errands to the more restful home environment. One way you can do this is by creating energetic movement. Allowing your garage to be a storehouse for in-progress projects creates a momentum in the space. As you're clearing things out of the garage, ask yourself, *Is this in progress or stuck?* Then remove the items that do not have a purpose and organize the things that might not be currently in use but will be eventually used (for example, the lawn mower in winter or the snow shovel in July).

To add even more Magic to this space, consider decorating your garage. Yes, that's allowed! You can even paint the inside walls a fun color. (Seriously, why don't we do this more?) Since the garage transitions you from the outside to the inside energy of your home, let the colors and decor reflect that! Choose white accents for cleansing, blue for peace, or black for protection.

Finally, if your garage is attached to the house, place a stick of selenite above the door or a bell on the handle to cleanse your energy as you enter and leave the home. You could also make a room spray for cleansing by mixing salt and cleansing herbs with moon water; place it by your entryway to clean your hands and shoes as you enter.

"Princess" parking

Parking can be intimidating, so why not turn it into a simple manifestation ritual that will help strengthen your clairvoyance at the same time? Princess parking is a practice of visualizing your perfect parking spot, as if you were being dropped off by a royal driver to your destination. Here's how to do it.

Before you leave the house, imagine driving to your destination. Visualize as best you can the parking lot or street you plan to park on. See yourself pulling into the perfect parking spot; feel a sense of assuredness that you will find the perfect spot at the right time.

Now head to your destination, release any expectation that you will find a parking spot, and allow the universe to deliver! You might surprise yourself with an even better spot than you could have imagined!

Washing the car

Since your garage is the transition between home and outside, your car is the vehicle for that transition—pun intended. Keeping the car clean purifies the energy that you pick up in your travels. It also makes Protection Magic more potent, which can help you feel more at ease in the car.

As you vacuum inside the car, imagine sucking up any energy you've picked up in your travels. The road rage you felt, the impatience while stuck in traffic, or any other pent-up stress energy from your commute home—suck that out with the crumbs and dirt.

As you wipe down inside your car, imagine you could wipe away any stress that you feel when driving. As you clean the windows, invite the energy of the sun or moon to purify the energy as it shines through them. When you wash the outside of your car, allow the water and soap to create a protective energetic coating around your vehicle, keeping you and your passengers safe.

Finally, once the car is clean, let's add some more Protection Magic! Spritz some Florida Water on the carpet to freshen the scent inside and to continue to cleanse the energy. Walk around the vehicle counterclockwise, flicking either moon water or Florida Water onto the car as you go, with the intention of banishing any harmful energies that may enter your space.

Place a sachet with black tourmaline, selenite, and amethyst in your car somewhere to help protect, cleanse, and calm the energy in your car.

Planning routine car maintenance

Depending on your car's needs, this could be a great solstice/equinox ritual. As you move into a new season of life, ensure the ride is smooth and efficient by scheduling your oil change and other routine maintenance. Now, as you wait for your car to be done, bring your journal and use this time to write down your intentions for the coming season. Think of this like setting your energetic GPS for the direction you want your life to take. Here are a few ideas to consider:

- What habits and routines do I need to implement to best align with my intentions this season?
- What mindset do I need to maintain? What do I need to release?
- Where can I see intention play out in my daily routines through Mundane Magic?

- What other chores or errands do I need to do this season? How can I infuse this intention into them?

As you drive off after your car maintenance appointment, feel the energy in your car and spirit refreshed with new direction for the season ahead!

Cleaning the grill

Utilize the element of fire to empower your spell work! As you scrub the grill, call on the fire to assist you in blazing a trail for your manifestations. Now use your kitchen witchery skills to make a spice blend for your intention to season your grillables (find inspiration in the Ingredients Appendix, page 291!). As you cook, reconnect with the fire element to fan the flames of your intention.

Power washing the house and walkways

Harness the element of water to blast away stagnant energy using your power washer. Water is associated with the flow of emotions. As you use the power of water to clear away dirt and debris from your home, imagine any sticky emotions leaving your mental and emotional space at the same time.

Buying or finding a home

When searching for the perfect home, take note of the spiritual signs you're receiving. There may be a specific color you associate with home, or a specific tree or plant that feels like family to you. For example, when my spouse and I got married, we themed the wedding around blue hydrangeas—our first home was the same beautiful blue color and that felt like a sign. When we moved to a new home years later, we felt that feeling of *This is our home.* And as soon as that feeling hit, I noticed a tiny blue hydrangea bush hidden around the side of the house, cementing our decision.

Buying a home is a huge decision, so don't knock your intuition as you're going through the process! If you're searching for a sign, consider looking at the plants around the houses you're viewing to see what energies they can bring to the home.

Here are a few spiritual meanings for some common plants you might find around your home:

PLANT	SPIRITUAL MEANING
Daffodil	Rebirth, hope, new beginnings
Fern	Family, new beginnings, good fortune
Hosta	Strength, tranquility, growth
Hydrangea	**Blue:** Peace, gratitude, patience **Pink:** Joy, harmony, love **Purple:** Gratitude, friendship, wealth **Green:** Rebirth, good fortune, prosperity **White:** Purity, grace, hope
Ivy	Protection, longevity, hope
Lily	New beginnings, rebirth, love
Maple tree	Protection, wisdom, strength
Oak tree	Strength, growth, wisdom
Palm tree	Tranquility, resilience, peace
Pine tree	Longevity, endurance, adaptability
Rhododendron	Peace, safety, healing
Rose	Love, peace, happiness

In addition to looking at the plants around the home, you can look to the numerology of the home to get a feel for its energy.

Take the house number and add the digits together, then add the digits of that number together until you have a single-digit number. For example, if your address is 2878 Magic Lane, you would add 2+8+7+8 to get 25, then add 2+5 to get 7. If you live in an apartment, add your apartment number to the house number.

Once you have a single digit, you can look up the spiritual meaning of the number. There are lots of different beliefs around the meanings behind numbers; here is just one interpretation:

NUMBER	SPIRITUAL MEANING
1	New beginnings, fresh energy, entering a new cycle
2	Balance, equilibrium, patience
3	Expansion, growth, potential
4	Stability, consistency
5	Power, spiritual wisdom
6	Harmony, security
7	Growth, victory
8	Transformation, eternity
9	Introspection, settling, ending a cycle

Burying St. Joseph

The exact origins of this practice are unknown. Some say European nuns of the Middle Ages started it by burying tokens of St. Joseph on the land of convents they wanted to buy. Others believe it was German carpenters who started the tradition of burying St. Joseph to sell their home faster. Either way, since the 1980s this has been a popular tradition for people of many faiths—while St. Joseph is traditionally honored in Catholic or Christian faiths, this practice has expanded beyond the confines of organized religion. That said, if working with a Christian deity causes you discomfort, feel free to adapt this practice to your own faith.

As the patron saint of home and family, St. Joseph is said to bring luck to real estate sales. Burying his statue is said to incentivize the saint to support the sale of your home in order for him to be freed and turned right side up again.

Purchase a small statue of St. Joseph when you need to sell your home. Bury him by the FOR SALE sign with his head down, facing your home. Repeat the following prayer, which has been adapted to fit all faiths, secular and nonsecular. Feel free to tweak it to fit your voice:

> St. Joseph, I am going to place you in an uncomfortable position, with your head in darkness until this [house/property] is sold. Then, St. Joseph, I swear before [God/the universe/my spirit team] that I will redeem you. You will receive my gratitude and a place of honor in my home.

To speed things up, add some coffee grounds before covering him up and repeat the prayer daily over your morning coffee. When your house sells, unbury St. Joseph, clean him off, and place him on your altar or in another place of reverence in your new home.

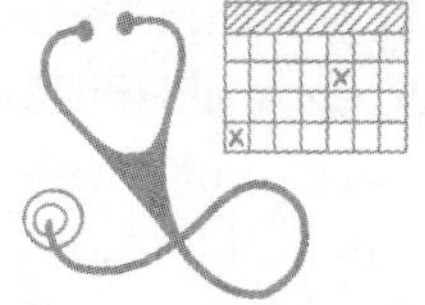

Dentist and doctors' appointments

Making doctors' appointments

Instead of making that dreaded phone call to make a doctor's appointment, turn it into a whole ritual for good health! Start by creating a simmer pot for good health (check out Simmer Pot Recipes and Ideas, page 315, in the appendix!) or a sigil for healing. Now call in the feeling of what it's like to be healthy: Can you feel that energy in your body? What kind of thoughts would you have if you were totally healthy? Light a white candle to call that intention toward you and seal in the spell by scheduling that doctor's appointment!

Attending dentist and doctors' appointments

Medical anxiety is extremely common, so if you avoid going to the doctor or dentist at all costs, know that you are not alone. A combination of Mundane Magic tools can help make these visits a little bit less stressful. For example, one of my students, Sasha (not her real name), had extreme dental anxiety. She would often toss and turn all night before an appointment and was known to cancel last minute due to her fear. When she did attend a routine cleaning, she'd leave with crescent-shaped nail marks on her palms from clenching her hands so hard. Sasha started adding more Mundane Magic into other areas of her life and—because how you do anything is how you do everything—she started to see that her fear response to the dentist was a part of her brain assuming she was going to be chased by a tiger.

Instead of reactively following that fear, she decided to use her breath to come back to herself. As she sat in the dentist's chair, she placed her hands on her legs and sent herself Reiki energy while repeating this mantra: *Just for this breath, I release worry*. Now, let's be real—she still doesn't love going to the dentist, but she's able to actually stick with her appointments and get through her visits with a lot less stress.

Vet appointments

No one loves going to the vet—your pet surely doesn't enjoy getting poked and prodded, and you probably don't love the expenses that come from these visits. However, regular vet visits are imperative to keep your pet healthy over the long term. To soften the sting of these visits, consider implementing Little Treat Magic for you and your pet. Perhaps that means a trip to the drive-thru afterward for a pup-cup and a latte for you. Or maybe you take your pet on a scenic drive through the neighborhood. Perhaps you treat yourself to extra snuggle time with your furry or feathered friend. Consider this a way to turn a not-so-fun errand into an opportunity to express gratitude for your pet's health and bond with them in the process!

Voting

Whether it's for a local or federal election, voting is an act of spiritual self-care and a manifestation ritual in and of itself. Voting is like writing a petition to the universe: you cast a physical and energetic ballot for the future you want for yourself and your community.

Before you receive your ballot, consider researching a sample ballot and printing it out. While you research, light an orange or white candle for empowerment while you imagine the life you want in one month, one year, five years . . . Which candidates or ballot measures align most closely with that vision? Fill out your sample ballot and place it on your altar. On top, place a carnelian crystal for power and quartz points facing out to direct that energy into your community.

On election day, consider wearing purple to denote royalty and empowerment. Perhaps you add an accessory or paint your nails the color that represents your candidates of choice.

Finally, voting can be an emotional experience. Give yourself time and space to celebrate or, if necessary, to grieve. If a candidate you disapprove of wins, don't let that disempower you. Instead, consider focusing on the interconnectedness of all beings everywhere. Where can you get involved in your community and make a difference despite the outcome of this election? How can you get involved in local politics to create togetherness when federal elections feel divisive? Use this energy of taking action to remind you of your own power.

Appendix

I hope *Mundane Magic* inspires you to enjoy your home, your to-do list, and your life a little bit more. I've added even more ingredients, Magical practices, and ideas to this appendix to help you on your journey. As always, take what resonates, use what you have—and remember YOU are the Magic!

Important note: Exposure to certain herbs and ingredients can be harmful to pets, so be sure to do additional research on your specific furry and feathered familiars before introducing new items to your space.

Chore Charts

New Moon Chore Chart

Full Moon Chore Chart

Solstice/Equinox Chore Chart

Make-Your-Own Checklists

Use the following charts to make your own Mundane Magic schedule. Each chart is organized by:

- **Daily Rituals:** Choose three to five things you will do daily to care for yourself, your space, and your Magic.
- **Magical Upkeep:** Choose one to two tasks per day of the week to keep your home and your energy feeling balanced.
- **Deep Magic:** Add in one to two Deep Magic tasks per week and rotate through them. You can consider adding in the full moon and new moon and using the blank chore charts to expand on these days as well.

Since the animal chores and personal care tasks are spread throughout the chapters, they've been added to page 282 to help you find them more easily. Consider adding a few to your checklist!

Daily Rituals

✦ Feel free to use all five spots ...or fewer! ✦

Take Medication	Drink Water	Tea Magic	Apply Sunscreen	Walk the Dog

Magical Upkeep

SUN	MON	TUE	WED	THU	FRI	SAT
Vacuum	Clutter Crushing Charm	Laundry Wash + Dry	Fold Laundry	Organize the Fridge	Grocery Shop	Clean the Bedsheets

Deep Magic

Shade and/or write in the moon phase

◐ ____	○ FULL!	◑ ____	● NEW
Dust Blinds	Clean the Shower Curtain Liner	Clean Baseboards	Meal Prep

Daily Rituals

Magical Upkeep

SUN	MON	TUE	WED	THU	FRI	SAT

Deep Magic

○___	○___	○___	○___

Animal chores

- ○ Decluttering pet toys (*page 77*)
- ○ Tending the animal cage (*page 90*)
- ○ Decorating the fish tank (*page 91*)
- ○ Feeding your pet and washing pet bowls (*page 125*)
- ○ Medication reminders for pets (*page 162*)
- ○ Nail trims for pets (*page 166*)
- ○ Scooping the litter box (*page 169*)
- ○ Bathing pets (*page 172*)
- ○ Cleaning pet bedding (*page 193*)
- ○ Removing bugs from your furry friends (*page 245*)
- ○ Walking the dog (*page 257*)
- ○ Picking up poop (*page 257*)
- ○ Vet appointments (*page 272*)

Personal care tasks

- ○ Checking in with your needs (*page 61*)
- ○ Exercise (*page 66*)
- ○ Stretching (*page 67*)
- ○ Eating three meals a day (*page 116*)
- ○ Drinking water (*page 123*)
- ○ Brushing your teeth and flossing (*page 152*)
- ○ Bathing, showering, and washing your hair (*page 153*)
- ○ Shaving (*page 157*)
- ○ Exfoliating (*page 158*)
- ○ Applying lotion (*page 160*)
- ○ Taking medication (*page 161*)
- ○ Washing your mouth guard or dentures (*page 162*)
- ○ Doing skincare (*page 163*)
- ○ Applying sunscreen (*page 164*)
- ○ Brushing your hair (*page 164*)
- ○ Nail care (*page 166*)
- ○ Going to bed on time (*page 180*)
- ○ Falling asleep (*page 184*)
- ○ Waking up early (*page 189*)
- ○ Getting dressed (*page 190*)

Ritual Bath Recipes

Measurements for each ingredient:

While there are no specific rules for how much of any one ingredient you should add to a ritual bath, here are a few guidelines to start from. Feel free to adjust based on the size of your bath, your preferences, and what you have on hand.

- **Fruit:** 3 to 4 slices, ¼ cup, or a fruit's worth of peelings (example: the peel of one orange)

- **Ground spices (examples: rosemary, lemon balm, cinnamon):** 1 teaspoon to 1 tablespoon, depending on your scent preferences
- **Chunky spices (examples: cloves, star anise, bay leaf):** 2 to 3 pieces or more, depending on your preferences
- **Flowers and herbs:** ⅛ to ¼ cup (these can be fresh or dried)
- **Epsom salt or oats:** ¼ cup

Make sure to add your ingredients to a sachet or sock to avoid making a mess of your bathtub!

ABUNDANCE

- **Oats** *for abundance*
- **Cinnamon** *for prosperity and luck*
- **Orange peel** *for joyful abundance*
- **Clove** *to protect your abundance*

CLEAR COMMUNICATION

- **Lemon balm** *for calm communication*
- **Mint** *for mental clarity*
- **Rosemary** *to stay grounded*
- **Epsom salt** *to protect and relax your body*

FULL MOON—CLEANSING

- **Lemon peel** *to cleanse your energy*
- **Lemon balm** *to calm*
- **Mint** *for clarity*
- **Epsom salt** *for release*

GRIEF

- **Lavender** *to relax the heart and invite in ease*
- **Lemon balm** *to dispel grief*
- **Oats** *to heal*
- **Salt** *to protect the heart*

HEALING (OATMEAL)

- **Oats** *for healing*
- **Calendula** *for positive energy*
- **Jasmine** *to heal the aura/energy field*

HEALING (SALT)

- **Lavender** *to heal the body*
- **Rosemary** *to heal the spirit*
- **Lemon balm** *to heal the mind*
- **Epsom salt** *to protect your body, spirit, and mind*

INTUITION ENHANCEMENT

- **Oats** *for grounding*
- **Mint** *for clarity*
- **Nutmeg** *to break through mental blocks*
- **Bay leaf** *for success*
- **Epsom salt** *for protection*

LUCK

- **Lilac** *to protect your luck*
- **Orange peel** *to brighten and lift your energy*
- **Star anise** *to tap into your intuition*
- **Oats** *to heal any wounds preventing your luck*

MONEY

- **Chamomile** *to enhance positive energy*
- **Calendula** *to call in abundance*
- **Bay leaf** *with the amount you wish to receive written on it*
- **Epsom salt** *to protect your investments*

NEW MOON—MANIFESTING

- **Bay leaf** *for success*
- **Orange peel** *for joy*
- **Jasmine** *for attraction*
- **Oats** *for healing*

PSYCHIC ABILITIES

- **Lavender** *to relax the mind*
- **Star anise** *to connect with your wisdom*
- **Lemon balm** *to clear away doubt*
- **Epsom salt** *to protect your energy*

ROAD OPENER

- **Nutmeg** *to break through obstacles*
- **Bay leaf** *for success*
- **Cinnamon** *for luck*
- **Mint** *for clarity*
- **Lemon** *to clear the path*
- **Epsom salt** *for protection*

SELF-LOVE

- **Rose** *for self-love*
- **Hibiscus** *for self-forgiveness*
- **Lavender** *for relaxation*
- **Pink Himalayan salt** *to protect the heart*

SWEET DREAMS

- **Mugwort** *for sleep*
- **Lavender** *for relaxation of body*
- **Jasmine** *for relaxation of mind*
- **Epsom salt** *for relaxation of body and protection of your energy*

Mopping Potions

ABUNDANCE

- **Cinnamon** *for prosperity*
- **Orange** *for joyful abundance*
- **Clove** *to protect your abundance*

ATTRACTING NEW OPPORTUNITIES

- **Cinnamon** *for luck*
- **Ginger** *to speed things up*
- **Mint** *to clarify the opportunity*

CLARITY

- **Mint** *for mental clarity*
- **Lemon balm** *to slow down*
- **Lemon** *for cleansing*

CLEANSING

- *Any citrus:* **lemon** *to cleanse and to banish negativity;* **orange** *to cleanse and to uplift;* **lime** *to cleanse and to relax*

CREATIVITY

- **Mint** *to clear the mind*
- **Lemon** *to clear stagnant energy*
- **Citrine** *for creativity*

EMBRACING CHANGE

- **Lemon** *for cleansing*
- **Eucalyptus** *for fresh energy*
- **Clove** *for grounding*

FOCUS

- **Mint** *for mental clarity*
- **Rosemary** *for memory*
- **Lavender** *to calm the mind*

GRIEF

- **Orange** *to reconnect with joy and to brighten*
- **Lavender** *to bring ease into the body*
- **Chamomile** *for rest*
- **Rose** *for heart healing*

GROUNDING

- **Clove** *to dispel fear*
- **Lemon** *to banish negativity and to cleanse*
- **Red jasper** *for grounding*

HEALING OR OVERCOMING SICKNESS

- **Lemon** *to cleanse and to protect from sickness*
- **Crack of black pepper** *to banish sickness*
- **Mint** *to clear passages, if the sickness includes congestion*
- **Lavender** *for soothing, if the sickness includes body aches*

JOY

- **Lemon** *to cleanse and to banish negativity*
- **Orange** *to uplift and to add joy*
- **Sunstone** *for happiness*

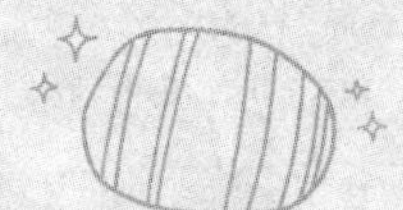

LOVE

- **Rose** *for self-love*
- **Hibiscus** *for attraction*
- **Jasmine** *for love*

MOTIVATION

- **Eucalyptus** *to bring fresh energy*
- **Mint** *to clear brain fog*
- **Orange** *to enjoy your work*

NEW YEAR OR NEW SEASON

- **Cherry blossom** *for fresh starts and rebirth*
- **Orange** *for joy*

PEACE

- **Lavender** *to calm*
- **Lemon balm** *for peaceful communication*

PROTECTION

- **Salt** *for protection*
- **Lemon** *to cleanse and to banish negativity*

ROAD OPENER

- **Nutmeg** *to break through obstacles*
- **Bay leaf** *for success*
- **Cinnamon** *for luck*
- **Mint** *for clarity*
- **Salt** *for protection*

SELF-LOVE

- **Rose** *for self-love*
- **Hibiscus** *for self-acceptance*
- **Basil** *to ward off negativity*

SELLING A HOME

- **Cinnamon** *for luck and prosperity*
- **Mint** *to help the buyer make a clear decision*
- **Calendula** *to invite in joy and abundance*
- **Salt** *for protection*
- **Rosemary** *to protect your time and to ensure that only buyers who are a good fit for your home set up showings*

Ingredients Appendix

INGREDIENT	MAGICAL PROPERTIES
Acorn	Prosperity, protection, luck
Allspice	Protection, energy, money, love
Almond	Money spells, prosperity, wisdom, success, banishing, grounding, clarity, abundance, healing
Aloe	Protection, healing, soothing, harmony
Apple	Money spells, healing, creativity, longevity, protection, love, abundance
Basil	Anti-anxiety, success, abundance, protection, love, luck
Bay leaf	Intuition, manifestation, success
Beet	Beauty, self-love, grounding
Black pepper	Protection, intuition, confidence
Black tea	Courage, focus, energy, protection
Blueberry	Protection, luck, abundance
Brazil nut	Grounding, love, balance
Brown sugar	Comfort, love, attraction
Butter	Anti-anxiety, soothing, peace, change, transitions, relationships, courage
Cardamom	Dispelling grief, attraction, courage, confidence, energy
Carrot	Passion, creativity, grounding, abundance
Cashew	Prosperity, love, communication
Cayenne	Speeding up spells, banishing, removing obstacles, energy, protection, passion

INGREDIENT	MAGICAL PROPERTIES
Celery	Anti-anxiety, intuition, sleep, mental clarity, protection, lust
Chamomile	Money spells, sleep, relaxation, meditation, purification, protection, success, abundance
Chestnut	Abundance, protection, warding
Chicory	Protection, focus, mental clarity, perseverance
Chili	Banishing, protection, cleansing
Chive	Blocking negativity, balance, strength
Cilantro	Peace, protection, healing
Cinnamon	Money spells, success, abundance, protection, luck, psychic powers, intuition
Clove	Money spells, protection, love, confidence, focus, healing, success, abundance
Cocoa	Grounding, focus, growth
Coconut	Confidence, strength, glamour
Coffee	Protection, grounding, luck, boosting energy, removing blockages, speeding up spells
Corn	Protection, luck, divination, abundance, prosperity, fertility
Cranberry	Protection, energy, communication, abundance, healing, courage
Cumin	Luck, protection, sleep, prosperity
Curry	Creativity, passion, courage, luck
Daffodil	Luck, resilience, abundance, love, friendship, regeneration
Dandelion	Wishes, manifestation, abundance, psychic abilities, growth, transformation
Dark chocolate	Grounding, love, positivity, joy, prosperity, emotional balance
Dill	Luck, passion, balance

INGREDIENT	MAGICAL PROPERTIES
Fennel	Purification, healing, protection, love, courage, home warding
Garden sage	Banishing, cleansing, wisdom, longevity, protection, wishes, purification, dispelling grief
Garlic	Protection, banishing, health
Ginger	Success, boosting energy, confidence, speeding up spells
Grapefruit	Focus, manifestation, psychic abilities
Grapeseed	Mental clarity, money, focus
Green tea	Energy, longevity, mental clarity, focus
Hazelnut	Abundance, self-love, wisdom, protection
Hibiscus	Love, passion, psychic abilities, attraction
Honey	Sweetness, attraction, productivity, prosperity, happiness, passion
Hydrangea	Rebirth, prosperity, renewal, grace, gratitude, apologies
Jalapeño	Growth, purification, protection
Jojoba	Love, emotional resilience
Lavender	Anti-anxiety, intuition, sleep, purification, dispelling grief, happiness, peace
Lemon	Purification, clarity, protection, happiness, friendship, new beginnings
Lemon balm	Calm, healing, dispelling grief
Lemongrass	Cleansing, transformation, mental clarity, grounding
Lettuce	Protection, grounding, sleep
Lime	Healing, peace, relaxation
Macadamia nut	Abundance, protection
Mango	Abundance, growth, happiness
Maple	Money spells, protection, love, longevity, tolerance, attraction, abundance

INGREDIENT	MAGICAL PROPERTIES
Marjoram	Dispelling grief, cleansing, purifying, protecting
Matcha	Clarity, mood, health
Milk	Abundance, prosperity, healing, beauty
Milk chocolate	Friendship, self-love, positivity, joy, prosperity, emotional balance
Mint	Money spells, protection, clarity, cleansing, healing, decision making, anti-anxiety, abundance, intuition, success, purification
Molasses	Energy, balancing, motivation, cleansing
Mustard seed	Protection, warding, healing
Nutmeg	Intuition, dream work, breaking through obstacles
Oats	Money spells, stability, grounding, happiness, spiritual growth, friendship, abundance
Olive	Anti-anxiety, peace, protection, healing, potency, luck
Onion	Protection, cleansing, banishing
Oolong	Wisdom, self-love, connection, intuition
Orange	Money spells, love, luck, joy, energy, divination, success, abundance
Oregano	Anti-anxiety, protection, creativity, happiness, love, abundance
Paprika	Energy, speeding up spells, protection, luck
Parsley	Protection, success, purification
Peanut	Stability, energy, manifestation
Peas	Love, money, protection
Pecan	Longevity, prosperity, purification, protection
Pine nut	Purification, prosperity, warding
Pineapple	Courage, luck, confidence
Pomegranate	Friendship, protection, wisdom, wishes, growth, new beginnings, luck

INGREDIENT	MAGICAL PROPERTIES
Poppy seed	Success, bravery, prosperity
Potato	Grounding, health, growth, protection
Pumpkin	Protection, longevity, letting go, abundance, prosperity, spirituality
Radish	Lust, protection, prosperity
Red pepper flakes	Luck, protection, banishing
Rhubarb	Protection, attraction, willpower
Rooibos	Stress relief, sleep, clarity, healing
Rose	Anti-anxiety, self-love, intuition, healing, protection, luck
Rosemary	Purification, abundance, protection, healing, sleep, intuition
Saffron	Love, healing, strength, psychic powers, happiness, abundance
Salt	Protection, cleansing, banishing, healing, success, purification
Sesame seed	Abundance, success, money
Shallot	Purification, luck
Soy	Banishing, spell enhancing, protection, spirituality, grounding, psychic awareness
Spinach	Growth, connection, strength, clarity, abundance
Star anise	Purification, intuition, luck, psychic abilities, protection, calming
Strawberry	Luck, self-love, dedication
Sugar	Sweetness, love, attraction, cleansing
Tarragon	Confidence, courage, calm, growth, healing, protection
Thyme	Courage, wisdom, intuition
Tomato	Abundance, prosperity, love, protection

INGREDIENT	MAGICAL PROPERTIES
Turmeric	Purification, love, health, protection
Vanilla	Anti-anxiety, happiness, passion, healing, mental clarity, love
Walnut	Abundance, healing, clarity, luck
White chocolate	Fun, self-love, positivity, purification, joy, prosperity
White tea	Cleansing, protection, mental clarity
Yard grass	Good luck, purification, protection, abundance, happiness, calming

Crystal Appendix

CRYSTAL	CAN HELP WITH
Amethyst	Intuition, relaxation, decision making
Ametrine	Peaceful communication
Apophyllite	Spiritual expansion, connection to spirit, intuition
Aqua aura quartz	Communication, dispelling anger
Aquamarine	Communication, intuition, alleviating seasickness
Aragonite	Clearing self-doubt, anti-anxiety
Black tourmaline	Sleep, grounding, reducing overwhelm, energy protection
Bloodstone	Grounding, healing, vitality
Blue kyanite	Peaceful communication
Blue lace agate	Loving-kindness, quieting overthinking, removing writer's block, peaceful communication, reducing overwhelm, sleep, anti-anxiety, relieving stress
Carnelian	Passion, motivation, creativity, removing writer's block, balancing menstruation, clearing self-doubt, health and fitness
Celestite	Sleep, balancing menstruation, relieving stress
Chrysocolla	Peaceful communication
Citrine	Energy, manifestation, removing writer's block, abundance, intuition, health and fitness
Clear quartz	Works for all intentions, intuition, amplification
Emerald	Self-love
Epidote	Heart healing, healing grief
Fluorite	Clarity, quieting overthinking, focus, decision making, energy protection
Garden quartz	Transformation, connection, grounding, clarity
Garnet	Success, safe travels, friendship, grounding, luck

CRYSTAL	CAN HELP WITH
Green aventurine	Heart healing, luck, abundance, clearing self-doubt
Hematite	Focus, grounding, attraction
Howlite	Relaxation, calm, balance
Jade	Abundance, luck
Jet	Travel, reducing overwhelm, energy protection, relieving stress, anti-anxiety
Labradorite	Intuition, energy protection
Lapis lazuli	Communication, clarity, truth
Lepidolite	Anti-anxiety, mood, relaxation
Malachite	Intuition, health and fitness
Moldavite	Transformation, expansion, removing obstacles
Moonstone	Intuition, balancing rest with action, spiritual awareness
Moss agate	Growth, grounding, nurturing the root
Obsidian	Grounding, inner-child healing, energy protection
Onyx	Grounding, focus
Orange calcite	Creativity, inspiration
Peridot	Relationships, luck, emotional support
Pyrite	Confidence, abundance, dispelling bad luck
Red jasper	Grounding, sleep, travel, removing worry
Rhodochrosite	Self-love
Rhodonite	Loving-kindness, self-love
Rose quartz	Loving-kindness, self-love, sleep, relieving stress
Selenite	Cleansing, intuition, travel, energy protection, relieving stress
Shungite	Grounding, protection, clarity
Smoky quartz	Sleep, quieting overthinking, removing writer's block, grounding, balancing menstruation, intuition, reducing overwhelm, anti-anxiety, relieving stress, removing worry

CRYSTAL	CAN HELP WITH
Snowflake obsidian	Grounding
Sodalite	Intuition, quieting overthinking, focus, decision making
Spirit quartz	Transformation, healing, spiritual growth
Sunstone	Creativity, joy, passion, travel, clearing self-doubt
Tiger's-eye	Confidence, decision making, balance

Ingredients by Intention

INTENTION	INGREDIENTS	CRYSTALS
Abundance	Almond, apple, basil, blueberry, carrot, chamomile, chestnut, cinnamon, clove, corn, cranberry, daffodil, dandelion, hazelnut, macadamia nut, mango, maple, mint, oats, orange, oregano, pumpkin, rosemary, saffron, walnut, yard grass	Citrine, green aventurine, jade, pyrite
Acceptance	Chamomile, garden sage, hibiscus, lavender, lemon balm, rose	Malachite, rose quartz
Anti-anxiety	Basil, butter, celery, lavender, mint, olive, oregano, rose, vanilla	Aragonite, blue lace agate, jet, smoky quartz
Attraction	Brown sugar, cardamom, hibiscus, honey, jasmine, maple, rhubarb, sugar	Citrine, hematite, rose quartz
Banishing	Almond, cayenne, garden sage, garlic, onion, salt, soy	Jet, obsidian, onyx
Beauty	Beet, rose, white tea	Jade, rose quartz
Becoming present	Green tea, lavender, mint	Garden quartz, garnet, moss agate
Blocking negativity	Basil, chili, chive, salt	Black tourmaline, jet, obsidian, shungite
Bravery	Ginger, poppy seed	Carnelian, citrine

INTENTION	INGREDIENTS	CRYSTALS
Breaking through obstacles	Cayenne, coffee, nutmeg	Clear quartz, fluorite, obsidian, selenite
Calm/relaxation	Chamomile, jasmine, lavender, mint, star anise, yard grass	Amethyst, blue lace agate, smoky quartz
Change	Agave, butter, dandelion	Malachite, spirit quartz
Clarity	Almond, celery, lemon, mint, vanilla, walnut	Amethyst, fluorite, sodalite
Cleansing	Garden sage, mint, onion, salt	Amethyst, clear quartz, selenite
Communication	Cashew, cranberry, mint	Ametrine, blue kyanite, blue lace agate, chrysocolla
Compassion	Hibiscus, jasmine, lavender, rose	Blue lace agate, rhodonite, rose quartz
Confidence	Black pepper, clove, coconut, ginger, pineapple	Aragonite, carnelian, citrine, green aventurine, green sunstone
Courage	Butter, cranberry, fennel, pineapple, thyme	Carnelian, sunstone, tiger's-eye
Creativity	Apple, carrot, cheese, nutritional yeast, oregano	Carnelian, citrine, sunstone
Decision making	Grapeseed, green tea, lemongrass, mint, vanilla, white tea	Amethyst, fluorite, sodalite, tiger's-eye

INTENTION	INGREDIENTS	CRYSTALS
Dream work	Lavender, nutmeg	Amethyst, black tourmaline, red jasper
Emotional balance	Brazil nut, brown sugar, chive, dark chocolate, dill, maple, milk chocolate	Amethyst, tiger's-eye
Energy	Cayenne, coffee, cranberry, ginger, green tea, orange, paprika, peanut	Carnelian, clear quartz, red jasper
Focus	Clove, grapefruit, mint, rosemary	Fluorite, hematite, onyx, sodalite
Friendship	Daffodil, lemon, milk chocolate, oats, pomegranate	Garnet, green aventurine, peridot
Gratitude	Hydrangea	Citrine, rose quartz, sunstone
Grief (easing/ healing)	Garden sage, lavender, lemon balm, marjoram, oats, orange	Epidote, green aventurine, rhodonite, rose quartz
Grounding	Almond, beet, Brazil nut, carrot, coffee, dark chocolate, lettuce, oats, soy	Black tourmaline, onyx, red jasper, smoky quartz, snowflake obsidian
Growth	Dandelion, mango, pomegranate	Moonstone, moss agate
Happiness	Honey, lavender, lemon, mango, oats, oregano, saffron, vanilla, yard grass	Citrine, sunstone

INTENTION	INGREDIENTS	CRYSTALS
Healing/health	Almond, aloe, apple, cilantro, clove, cranberry, fennel, garlic, lime, mint, olive, rose, rosemary, saffron, salt, turmeric, vanilla, walnut	Citrine, malachite, red jasper
Intuition	Bay leaf, black pepper, celery, cinnamon, lavender, mint, nutmeg, rose, rosemary, star anise, thyme	Apophyllite, aquamarine, citrine, clear quartz, labradorite, malachite, selenite, smoky quartz
Joy	Dark chocolate, milk chocolate, orange, white chocolate	Citrine, sunstone
Longevity	Apple, garden sage, maple, pecan, pumpkin	Clear quartz, moonstone, moss agate
Love	Apple, basil, Brazil nut, cashew, clove, daffodil, dark chocolate, fennel, maple, orange, oregano, peas, saffron, turmeric, vanilla	Blue lace agate, rhodonite, rose quartz
Luck	Acorn, basil, blueberry, cinnamon, coffee, corn, daffodil, dill, olive, orange, pineapple, pomegranate, rose, shallot, star anise, strawberry, walnut, yard grass	Citrine, green aventurine, jade, pyrite
Manifestation	Bay leaf, dandelion, grapefruit, peanut	Citrine, green aventurine, jade, pyrite
Meditation	Black tea, chamomile, lavender, mint	Amethyst, clear quartz, fluorite

INTENTION	INGREDIENTS	CRYSTALS
Menstruation (balancing/ easing)	Hibiscus, raspberry leaf	Carnelian, red jasper, smoky quartz
Money	Almond, apple, calendula, chamomile, cinnamon, clove, maple, mint, oats, orange, peas	Citrine, jade, pyrite
Motivation	Chamomile, coffee, ginger, lemon	Citrine, garnet, green aventurine, tiger's-eye
New beginnings	Lemon, pomegranate	Malachite, moonstone
Overthinking (quieting)	Chamomile, jasmine, lavender, mint	Blue lace agate, fluorite, smoky quartz, sodalite
Overwhelm (reducing)	Chamomile, jasmine, lavender, orange, rose	Blue lace agate, jet, smoky quartz
Passion	Carrot, cayenne, dill, honey, vanilla	Carnelian, sunstone
Peace	Butter, cilantro, lavender, lime, olive	Amethyst, blue lace agate, rose quartz
Positivity	Dark chocolate, milk chocolate, white chocolate	Citrine, sunstone
Productivity	Coffee, ginger, honey	Carnelian, citrine, fluorite
Prosperity	Acorn, almond, cashew, corn, dark chocolate, honey, hydrangea, milk chocolate, pecan, pine nut, poppy seed, pumpkin, radish, white chocolate	Citrine, green aventurine, jade, peridot, pyrite

INTENTION	INGREDIENTS	CRYSTALS
Protection	Acorn, aloe, apple, basil, black pepper, blueberry, cayenne, celery, chamomile, chestnut, cilantro, cinnamon, clove, coffee, corn, cranberry, fennel, garden sage, garlic, hazelnut, lemon, lettuce, macadamia nut, maple, mint, olive, onion, oregano, parsley, peas, pecan, pomegranate, pumpkin, radish, rhubarb, rose, rosemary, salt, soy, star anise, turmeric, yard grass	Black tourmaline, fluorite, jet, labradorite, obsidian, selenite
Psychic powers/ abilities	Cinnamon, dandelion, grapefruit, saffron, star anise, soy	Amethyst, apophyllite, clear quartz, sodalite
Purification	Chamomile, fennel, garden sage, lavender, lemon, mint, parsley, pecan, pine nut, rosemary, salt, shallot, star anise, turmeric, white chocolate, yard grass	Amethyst, clear quartz, selenite
Reclaiming your energy	Cinnamon, coffee, lemon, salt	Black tourmaline, bloodstone, carnelian, citrine, selenite, tiger's-eye
Release	Grapefruit, lemon, pumpkin, salt	Black tourmaline, selenite, smoky quartz
Self-love	Beet, hazelnut, milk chocolate, rose, strawberry, white chocolate	Emerald, rhodochrosite, rhodonite, rose quartz

INTENTION	INGREDIENTS	CRYSTALS
Sleep	Celery, chamomile, lavender, lettuce, lime, rosemary	Black tourmaline, blue lace agate, red jasper, rose quartz, smoky quartz
Speeding up spells	Cayenne, coffee, ginger	Clear quartz
Spiritual growth	Pumpkin, soy, oats	Clear quartz, selenite
Stability	Oats, peanut	Black tourmaline, red jasper
Strength	Chive, coconut, daffodil, saffron	Carnelian, red jasper
Stress relief	Chamomile, jasmine, lavender, mint	Blue lace agate, carnelian, jet, rose quartz, selenite, smoky quartz
Success	Almond, basil, bay leaf, chamomile, cinnamon, clove, ginger, mint, orange, parsley, poppy seed, salt	Citrine, green aventurine, jade, pyrite
Tolerance	Hibiscus, lemon balm, maple, peppermint	Aquamarine, blue lace agate, green aventurine, howlite
Transformation	Butter, dandelion	Labradorite, malachite, moldavite
Warding	Chestnut, fennel, pine nut, salt	Black tourmaline, obsidian, onyx, selenite

INTENTION	INGREDIENTS	CRYSTALS
Wisdom	Almond, garden sage, hazelnut, pomegranate, thyme	Amethyst, lapis lazuli, sodalite
Wishes	Bay leaf, dandelion, garden sage, pomegranate	Citrine, jade

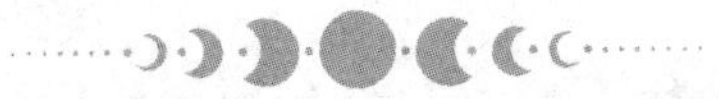

Easy Food Spells

Thai Cucumber Money Spell

INGREDIENTS:

- 1 cucumber
- 1 tablespoon peanut butter *so money sticks to you with ease*
- 1 teaspoon soy sauce *for grounding to stay humble*
- 1 teaspoon sesame oil *for abundance*
- 2 cloves garlic, minced, *to banish any debts*
- Pinch of salt *for protection*

INSTRUCTIONS:

- Slice the cucumber thinly and add to a bowl. Add the rest of the ingredients and stir to combine. Serve cold.

Elote Corn Protection Spell

INGREDIENTS:

- **One 10-ounce package of frozen corn** *for abundance of protection*
- **2 teaspoons sugar** *to replace the energy with sweetness*
- **1 teaspoon ground cumin** *for protection*
- **1½ teaspoons smoky paprika** *to energize the spell*
- **1 teaspoon salt** *for protection*
- **1 teaspoon each garlic powder** *and* **onion powder** *for banishing*
- **2 tablespoons chili powder** *to cut any connection with other people's negative energy*
- **½ cup mayonnaise** *for healing (add more or less based on your preferences)*

INSTRUCTIONS:

- Heat the corn up in the microwave according to package instructions. While the corn heats up, stir together the sugar, cumin, paprika, salt, garlic powder, onion powder, and chili in a bowl. Remove the corn from the microwave and add it and the mayonnaise to the spice mixture; stir to combine. Adjust the level of seasoning based on your preferences.

Egg Salad for Abundance

INGREDIENTS:

- **4 eggs** *to create abundance in your life*
- **Splash of vinegar**
- **¼ to ½ cup mayonnaise** *for healing*
- **¼ cup chopped celery** *for clarity*
- **1 tablespoon mustard** *for mental power to create abundance in your life*
- **1 tablespoon fresh dill** *for calling in that abundance*
- *To taste:* **salt** *and* **pepper** *to protect your abundance*
- **¼ cup chopped onion** *to banish anything blocking your abundance*
- **Lettuce leaves** *or* **sliced bread** *to serve*

INSTRUCTIONS:

- Hard-boil the eggs with a splash of vinegar in the water to banish debt and make the shells easier to peel. Once cooked, immediately place them in a bowl of ice water to cool. Peel the eggs and chop them. Place in a bowl then add the other ingredients to taste and stir to combine. Serve on lettuce leaves or your favorite bread.

Cinnamon Apple Oatmeal for Healing

INGREDIENTS:

- **½ cup quick-cooking oats** *for soothing any emotional wounds*
- **1 cup water** *or* **milk** *of your choice*
- **1 apple diced finely** *for self-love*
- **1 tablespoon brown sugar** *for emotional balance*
- **Pinch of salt** *for protection*
- **Pinch of cinnamon** *for luck*

INSTRUCTIONS:

- Mix all ingredients in a microwave-safe bowl. Microwave according to package instructions until all liquid is absorbed and the apples are slightly tender. Let cool for one minute and enjoy.

Coffee syrups

These syrups can be used in coffee or to add flavor and Magic to oatmeal, desserts, pancakes, and other dishes.

Churro Syrup for Abundance

INGREDIENTS:

- **2 cups hot water**
- **2 cups brown sugar** *for comfort around abundance*
- **3 cinnamon sticks** *for prosperity and luck*

INSTRUCTIONS:

- Dissolve the brown sugar in the hot water. Add the cinnamon sticks and let them infuse in the syrup for at least one hour; the longer they sit, the more cinnamony the syrup will be.

Peppermint Mocha for Clarity

INGREDIENTS:

- **2 cups hot water**
- **2 cups sugar**
- **¼ cup cocoa powder** *for grounding*
- **½ teaspoon** *to* **1 teaspoon peppermint extract** *for clear thinking (measure to taste)*

INSTRUCTIONS:

- Dissolve the sugar in the hot water, then add the cocoa and whisk until combined. Add in peppermint extract to taste.

Simmer Pot Recipes and Ideas

Measurements for each ingredient:

While there are no specific rules for how much of any one ingredient you should add to a simmer pot, here are a few guidelines to start from. Feel free to adjust based on the size of your simmer pot and what you have on hand.

- **Fruit:** 3 to 4 slices, ¼ cup, or a fruit's worth of peelings (example: the peel of one orange)
- **Ground spices (examples: ginger, cinnamon) and salt:** 1 teaspoon to 1 tablespoon, depending on your scent preferences
- **Chunky spices (examples: cloves, star anise, bay leaf):** 2 to 3 pieces or more, depending on your preferences

- **Flowers and herbs:** ⅛ to ¼ cup (these can be fresh or dried)

Be sure to set a timer and check your simmer pot often.

ABUNDANCE

- Orange
- Apples
- Cinnamon
- Calendula flowers
- Salt

BANISH SICKNESS

- Lemon
- Orange
- Cloves
- Cinnamon
- Salt

BLAH/EXHAUSTED

- **Orange peel** *for energy*
- **Cloves** *for focus*
- **Vanilla** *for mental clarity*
- **Salt**

BUST OUT OF A RUT

- **Lemon** *to clear the energy*
- **Orange** *to brighten the energy*
- **Pine** *to purify the space*
- **Mint** *to bring clarity and focus*
- **Salt** *for protection*

CHILL

- Vanilla
- Chamomile
- Cinnamon
- Salt

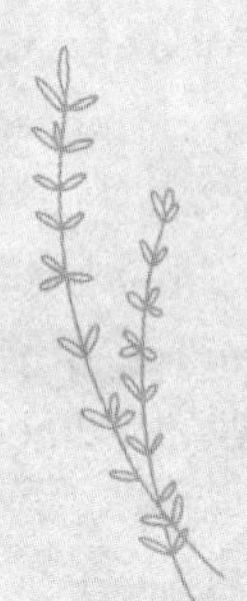

CLEANSE AND DE-STRESS

- Lemon
- Chamomile
- Rosemary
- Salt

CLEAR THINKING

- Mint
- Lemon
- Cloves
- Salt

CLEARING BLOCKED OR STAGNANT ENERGY

- Lemon
- Rosemary
- Eucalyptus or mint
- Salt

CONCENTRATION

- Cloves
- Rosemary
- Vanilla
- Red apples
- Salt *for protection*

CONFIDENCE

- Apples
- Cloves
- Orange
- Salt

CREATIVITY

- Lemon
- Mint
- Cinnamon
- Salt

DOWN ON YOUR LUCK

- **Rosemary** *to clear the path*
- **Rose** *for heart healing and kindness*
- **Orange** *for luck and brightening energy*
- **Salt**

EMOTIONAL SUPPORT

- Lavender
- Lemon
- Orange
- Mint
- Salt

ENERGY

- Ginger
- Orange
- Lemon
- Coffee

EQUINOX

- Lemon
- Orange
- Cloves
- Rosemary
- Salt

FOCUS

- Mint
- Rosemary
- Cloves
- Lemon
- Salt

FRESH START/REBIRTH

- Lemon
- Apples
- Cloves
- Cranberry

FULL MOON POT FOR WHEN YOU NEED HELP WITH GROUNDING

- Cloves
- Star anise
- Cinnamon
- Pear
- Salt

FULL MOON POT TO ASSIST WITH RELEASING/LETTING GO

- **Bay leaves** *(write what you want to release on them and crumple them in)*
- **Lemon** *for clear energy*
- **Cinnamon** *for luck*
- **Salt**

GET YOUR SHIT TOGETHER (MOTIVATION)

- Peppermint
- Eucalyptus
- Orange
- Salt

GOOD HEALTH

- Orange
- Cloves
- Cinnamon
- Rosemary
- Salt

GRIEF

- **Orange** *to reconnect with joy and to brighten*
- **Lavender** *to bring ease into the body*
- **Chamomile** *for rest*
- **Rose petals** *for heart healing*
- **Hibiscus** *for self-love (optional)*
- **Salt**

GRUMP DAYS

- Lemon
- Orange
- Green apples
- Rosemary
- Bay leaf
- Salt

HEALING ROOT CHAKRA FOR GROUNDING

- Rosemary
- Ginger
- Lemon
- Cloves *to dispel fear*
- Salt

HEALTH

- Orange
- Cloves
- Rosemary
- Cinnamon
- Salt

HOLIDAY GROUNDING

- Cranberry *(or any red fruit)*
- Rosemary
- Chamomile *or* lavender
- Cloves
- Salt

INTUITION

- Star anise
- Lavender
- Mint
- Lime
- Salt

MANIFESTATION

- Lemon
- Orange
- Cinnamon
- Bay leaf
- Salt
- Moon water *(optional)*

MERCURY IN RETROGRADE

- Orange
- Lemon
- Lavender
- Chamomile
- Rose petals
- Rosemary
- Salt

MOTIVATION

- Lemon
- Chamomile
- Ginger
- Salt

NEW HOME

- Lemon
- Cloves
- Cinnamon
- Bay leaves
- Salt

NEW MOON POT FOR EMPOWERMENT

- **Rosemary**
- **Mint**
- **Mango** *(or ginger or lemon)*
- **Salt**

NEW MOON POT FOR MANIFESTING

- **Lemon**
- **Orange**
- **Cinnamon**
- **Bay leaf** *(write what you want to manifest)*
- **Salt**

OVERWHELM

- **Lavender** *for calm*
- **Orange** *to brighten energy*
- **Salt**

PEACE

- **Chamomile**
- **Lavender**
- **Mint**
- **Orange**
- **Salt**

PMS

- **Orange**
- **Relaxing tea**
- **Salt**

PROCRASTINATION

- **Orange** *for energy*
- **Lavender** *to be nice to yourself*
- **Peppermint** *for focus*
- **Salt**

PROTECTING YOUR ENERGY

- **Grapefruit** *to lift stagnant energy*
- **Lemon** *to cleanse and purify*
- **Rosemary** *for grounding*
- **Activated charcoal** *to detoxify and protect your energy*
- **Cloves** *for courage*
- **Salt**

REBIRTH/FRESH STARTS

- Lemon
- Apples
- Cloves
- Cranberry
- Salt

REENERGIZING

- Orange
- Cranberry
- Cinnamon
- Ginger
- Salt

RELAXATION

- Orange peels
- Leftover relaxing tea
- Lavender
- Salt

ROAD OPENER

- **Nutmeg** *to break through obstacles*
- **Bay leaf** *for success*
- **Cinnamon** *for luck*
- **Mint** *for clarity*
- **Lemon** *to clear the path*
- **Salt** *for protection*

SELF-LOVE

- Jasmine flowers
- Rose petals
- Orange
- Salt

SELLING A HOME

- **Lemon** *to help the potential buyers make a clear offer*
- **Orange** *to infuse the space with joyful energy*
- **Salt** *to protect your investment and energy*
- **Cloves** *to give the potential buyers confidence in the purchase*
- **Cinnamon** *for abundance, luck, and prosperity*

SIMMER DOWN (DECREASE ANGER)

- Blue food coloring
- Chamomile
- Rosemary
- Rose petals
- Lavender
- Salt

SLEEP

- Rosemary
- Lavender
- Mint
- Salt

SPRING CLEANING MOTIVATION

- Lavender
- Orange
- Salt

STABILITY DURING BIG LIFE TRANSITIONS

- Chamomile *for ease*
- Cinnamon *for good luck*
- Cloves *for courage*
- Orange *for joy*
- Salt

STRESS RELIEF (END OF YEAR)

- Relaxing tea
- Orange juice
- Salt

WINTER SOLSTICE

- Lemon
- Orange
- Rosemary
- Cinnamon
- Salt

Acknowledgments

Back in 2008 I carried around a DIY wallet made from caution tape and in it was my "bucket list"—a collection of things I wanted to accomplish before I left this plane of existence. On it were things that felt important to me at that time, like owning a T-Mobile Sidekick (if you know, you know) and touring with a rock band. Many of those items have been long forgotten, but one stayed on every vision board or list of goals since: publish a book. About what or when, I never knew; I just knew it needed to happen. These are the folks who made it possible:

To my students and graduates—I had to list you first because without you, this book wouldn't exist. Whether you've trained with me or simply liked a post of mine on Instagram, YOU are the reason *Mundane Magic* is in this world. Thank you for supporting me, offering ideas and suggestions, laughing at my jokes, and generally cheering me on every damn day. I am forever grateful to be on this journey with you all.

To Madison Lillian—my podcast co-host, partner in crime, the Elphaba to my Glinda, and my bestie for life. Thank you for helping me uncover my Magic, encouraging me to take up space, and having my back literally always.

To Sarah Soggs—my healer, mentor, and truly the only one who saw my full spectrum from skepticism to where I am today. Thank you for helping me grow, evolve, and expand. You bring so much light to the world, your ripple effect is incredible, and I am forever inspired by you and all the ways you own your Magic.

To my spouse, Justin Richard, who encourages me to follow my Magic despite being a Virgo Skeptic who doesn't understand it at all. Thank you for always believing in me.

To Alaina "Naenae" Borst, who did the fantastic illustrations in this book. When we met in fifth grade, I never believed we'd actually publish a book together, and I'm pretty sure there are some high school teachers who would be in complete shock and disbelief if they saw this book. Thanks for reading my mind and for bringing my wacky ideas to life for literally twenty-plus years.

To my fabulous agent, Margaret Danko, thanks for sliding into my DMs and making this dream a reality. Seriously, this book would still be living in the recesses of my mind without your push to put it out into the world. I am forever grateful that YOU found ME and were a perfect fit from day one!!

My amazing editor, Katherine Leak, who from day one saw the Magic within these pages. Thanks for believing in my vision and bringing it to life!!

This book also wouldn't exist without Jade Omardeen, who somehow organizes the chaos of my brain and took every admin task off my plate so I could actually write this thing. My parents, Karen Aagesen, Terry Donlan, and Steve Feinberg, for believing in me and telling me to chase my dreams since I could walk. My teachers: Sagel Urlacher, Jacqui Bonwell, Krista Mitchell, and Katie Beane, who introduced me to the practices that inspired this book and encourage my curiosity.

Thank you to: Chris Byrne, Drew Soucy, Jo Seal, Zach Kang, Angie Machado, Lily Hazel, Michelle Montes Gardes, Piper Richard, June Richard, Jennifer Turner, Danielle Connor, Jenna Harding, Bryan Donlan, Justin Moore, MJ Mayes, Sara Loretta, Megan & Johan, Evy & Shy Feinberg, Jacqui Acree, Anna Seirian, Anthony Leitz, Jess Fairclough, Brittni Bonville, Tran Truong, Chelsee Joel, Amanda MacLeod, Lindsey Hicks, Woodie, Hercules, and to YOU for reading these words!!

Index

About the Author

Molly Donlan is a Reiki Master Teacher, crystal healing expert, yoga teacher, and co-host of the *Demystify Magic* podcast who has dedicated her life to helping others unlock the transformative power of energy work and alternative healing modalities. With a background as an advocate for survivors of sexual violence and as a former skeptic of all things woo, Molly emphasizes the importance of trauma-informed care while teaching through a blend of science and spirituality. Her approach is lighthearted and grounded in practicality, because life is stressful enough and these practices are meant to reduce the stress of life, not add to it!

mollydonlan.com
Instagram: @m0dizzl3
TikTok: @m0dizzl3